The XXL Keto Diet Cookbook

2000 Days of Flavorful and Wholesome Low-Carb and High-Fat Recipes to Boost Your Energy

Debra P. Johnson

Copyright© 2024 By Debra P. Johnson Rights Reserved

This book is copyright protected. It is only for personal use. You cannot amend, distribute, sell, use, quote or paraphrase any part of the content within this book, without the consent of the author or publisher.

Under no circumstances will any blame or legal responsibility be held against the publisher, or author, for any damages, reparation, or monetary loss due to the information contained within this book, either directly or indirectly.

Disclaimer Notice:

Please note the information contained within this document is for educational and entertainment purposes only. All effort has been executed to present accurate, up to date, reliable, complete information. No warranties of any kind are declared or implied. Readers acknowledge that the author is not engaged in the rendering of legal, financial, medical or professional advice. The content within this book has been derived from various sources. Please consult a licensed professional before attempting any techniques outlined in this book.

By reading this document, the reader agrees that under no circumstances is the author responsible for any losses, direct or indirect, that are incurred as a result of the use of the information contained within this document, including, but not limited to, errors, omissions, or inaccuracies.

Editor: AALIYAH LYONS

Interior Design: BROOKE WHITE

Cover Art: DANIELLE REES

Food stylist: SIENNA ADAMS

Table Of Contents

Introduction	1
Chapter 1	
Fueling Your Keto Journey	2
What is the Ketogenic Diet?	3
Getting Started with Keto	3
What To Eat and What To Avoid	5
Common Keto Mistakes	7
Chapter 2	
4-Week Meal Plan	9
Week 1	10
Week 2	10
Week 3	11
Week 4	11
Chapter 3	
Breakfast	13
Blackberry-Chia Pudding	14
Chocolate Hemp Smoothie	14
Almond Butter Smoothie	14
Cross-Country Scrambler	15
Creamy Coconut Porridge	15
Pineapple Ginger Smoothie	15
Liver Sausages & Onions	16

Creamy Cheddar Deviled Eggs	16
Mushroom & Cheese Lettuce Wraps	17
Bacon & Cheese Pesto Mug Cakes	17
Grain-Free Hemp Seed Porridge	18
Almond Waffles with Cinnamon Cream	18
Spicy Breakfast Scramble	19
Fontina Cheese and Chorizo Waffles	19
Cream Cheese Pancakes	19
Early-Day Jambalaya	20
Keto Breakfast Pudding	20
Spicy Eggs with Turkey Ham	21
Ginger & Walnut Porridge	21
Indian Masala Omelet	21
Sausage Breakfast Stacks	22
Sausage and Greens Hash Bowl	22
Grilled Halloumi Cheese with Eggs	23
Coconut Chai Vanilla Smoothie	23
Bacon Lovers' Quiche	24
Double-Pork Frittata	25
Eggs Benedict	25
Chimichurri Steak Bunwiches	26
Cacao Coconut Granola	26
Pepper Sausage Fry	27
Crêpes with Lemon-Buttery Syrup	27

Chapter 4
Snacks and Appetizers — 28

Coconut Flour Cheese Crackers	29
Skinny Cocktail Meatballs	29
Radish Chips & Cheese Bites	30
Baked Zucchini Gratin	30
Mug Biscuit	31
Homemade Dairy Kefir	31
Cheddar & Cream Cheese Chicken Casserole	31
Lemon Coconut Cheesecake Fat Bombs	32
Favorite Onions Rings	32
Chocolate Pistachio Truffles	32
Cultured Red Onion Relish	33
Classic Blueberry Cheesecake	33
Chia Protein Smoothie Bowl	34
Caribbean-Style Chicken Wings	34
Walnut and Seed Crunch Bars	34
Roasted Radishes with Brown Butter Sauce	35
Herbed Kefir Cheese	35
Cheesy Chips with Avocado Dip	36
Cauliflower and Broccoli Cakes with Cheese	36
Cheese and Bacon Fat Bombs	36
Spicy Roasted Pumpkin Seeds	37
Vanilla Custard Pudding	37
Fried Artichokes with Pesto	38
Parmesan and Pork Rind Green Beans	38
Golden Flax Seed and Pecan Pudding	38
Spanish Piquillo Peppers with Cheese Stuffing	39
Buttery Slow-Cooker Mushrooms	39
No-Bake Cheesecake Truffles	39

Chapter 5
Poultry — 40

Buttery Garlic Chicken	41
Parmesan Baked Chicken	41
Sauced Chicken Legs with Vegetables	42
Baked Zucchini with Chicken and Cheese	42
Teriyaki Chicken Wings with Spring Onions	43
Turkey Stew with Salsa Verde	43
Delicious Chicken Puttanesca	44
Creamy Stuffed Chicken with Parma Ham	44
Fried Chicken with Coconut Sauce	45
Creamy Slow-Cooker Chicken	45
Cheesy Turkey Sausage Egg Muffins	45
Italian-Seasoned Turkey Breasts	46
Chicken with Parmesan Topping	46
Traditional Hungarian Paprikash	47
Baked Garlic and Paprika Chicken Legs	47
Tangy Classic Chicken Drumettes	48
Paprika Chicken Sandwiches	48
Cheddar Chicken Tenders	49
Chicken Cauliflower Bake	49
Crunchy Chicken Milanese	50
Zesty Grilled Chicken	50
Chicken with Monterey Jack Cheese	51
Cheesy Bacon and Broccoli Chicken	51
Grilled Chicken with Broccoli & Carrots	52
Creamy Mushroom & White Wine Chicken	52

Chapter 6
Beef, Lamb and Pork — 53

- Leek & Beef Bake — 54
- Kalua Pork with Cabbage — 54
- Thyme Beef & Bacon Casserole — 55
- Mexican-Inspired Beef Chili — 55
- Pork Chops with Raspberry Sauce — 55
- Classic Italian Bolognese Sauce — 56
- Citrus Pork with Sauteed Cabbage & Tomatoes — 56
- Green Chimichurri Sauce with Pork Steaks — 56
- Grilled Sirloin Steak with Sauce Diane — 57
- Cauli Rice with Vegetables and Beef Steak — 57
- Mind-Blowing Burgers — 58
- Blue Cheese Pork Chops — 59
- Chili-Stuffed Avocados — 59
- Ground Beef Stew with Majoram & Basil — 60
- Beef Roast with Serrano Pepper Gravy — 60
- Pork Burgers with Sriracha Mayo — 60
- Beef Skewers with Ranch Dressing — 61
- Steak with Tallow Herb Butter — 61
- Traditional Bolognese Sauce with Zoodles — 62
- Slow-Cooker Barbecue Ribs — 62
- Cabbage & Sausage with Bacon — 62
- Bombay Sloppy Jolenes — 63
- Cheesy Meatballs & Noodles — 63

Chapter 7
Fish and Seafood — 64

- Homemade Lobster Salad Rolls — 65
- Greek Salad with Grilled Salmon — 65
- Parmesan-Crusted Salmon Bake with Asparagus — 66
- Shrimp Fry — 66
- Niçoise Salad with Seared Tuna — 67
- Baked Cod with Parmesan and Almonds — 67
- Mediterranean-Style Halibut Fillets — 68
- Spicy Tuna Cakes — 68
- The Best Sardine Burgers Ever — 68
- Low-Carb Crab Cakes — 69
- Fresh Tilapia Omelet with Goat Cheese — 69
- Crab Tacos — 70
- Smoked Salmon Stacks — 70
- Sea Bass with Dijon Butter Sauce — 71
- Crispy Salmon Steaks with Sweet Cabbage — 71

Chapter 8
Vegan and Vegetarian — 72

- Herbed Pumpkin — 73
- Tofu & Vegetable Stir-Fry — 73
- Simple Spaghetti Squash — 73
- Kale with Bacon — 74
- Golden Mushrooms — 74
- Marinated Portobello Mushrooms — 74
- Cheesy Cauliflower Puree — 75
- Hot Pizza with Tomatoes, Cheese & Olives — 75
- Secret Stuffed Peppers — 76
- Greek Salad with Poppy Seed Dressing — 76
- Sweet-Braised Red Cabbage — 77
- Mozzarella & Bell Pepper Avocado Cups — 77
- Smoked Vegetable Bake with Parmesan — 78
- Sweet Sesame Glazed Bok Choy — 78

Chapter 9
Soups, Stew and Salads — 79

- Chinese Tofu Soup — 80
- Spanish-Style Tomato Soup — 80
- Creamy Coconut Soup with Chicken & Celery — 80
- Cowboy Stew of Bacon, Cheese & Cauliflower — 81
- Baked Winter Pork Stew — 81
- Awesome Chicken Enchilada Soup — 82
- Creamy Broccoli and Bacon Soup — 82
- Zucchini and Shallot Soup — 83
- Grilled Tofu Kabobs with Arugula Salad — 83
- Caprese Asparagus Salad — 84
- Cilantro Shrimp Stew with Sriracha Sauce — 84
- Stewed Turkey with Greens — 84
- Almond Parsnip Soup with Sour Cream — 85
- Cream of Cauliflower & Leek Soup — 85
- Creamy Roasted Asparagus Salad — 85
- Three-Color Salad with Pesto Sauce — 86

Grandma's Chicken Soup	86	Appendix 1 Measurement Conversion Chart	88
Asian-Style Turkey Soup	86		
Red Wine & Pork Stew	87	Appendix 2 The Dirty Dozen and Clean Fifteen	89
Mushroom Cream Soup with Herbs	87		
Old-Fashioned Chicken Salad	87	Appendix 3 Index	90

Introduction

Welcome to a journey of discovery, as we delve into the transformative world of the ketogenic diet. This is not just a guide; it's an invitation to explore a lifestyle that has captivated many on the path to improved health and well-being.

The ketogenic diet, often referred to as "keto," isn't just a trend; it's a science-backed approach to eating that has garnered attention for its potential benefits. As you turn the pages ahead, you'll uncover the foundations of keto – an understanding of macronutrients, the science behind ketosis, and the practicalities of incorporating keto-friendly foods into your daily life.

Consider this foreword as your introduction to the core principles that underpin the ketogenic lifestyle. This journey goes beyond the plate, offering insights into how the choices we make in our daily nutrition can have a profound impact on our overall health.

As you delve into the pages that follow, envision this foreword as a compass guiding you through the intricacies of the ketogenic lifestyle. Beyond the confines of a mere diet, keto is a philosophy—a science-backed philosophy—that reshapes our relationship with nutrition and, consequently, our bodies.

The ketogenic diet revolves around a simple yet profound idea: by altering our macronutrient intake, we can prompt the body to enter a state of ketosis. This metabolic state, characterized by the utilization of fats for energy, opens a door to a cascade of potential benefits—from weight management to increased mental clarity.

So, embark with an open mind, absorb the knowledge that follows, and may this exploration into the ketogenic world be a stepping stone to a healthier, more vibrant you. Welcome to the beginning of your journey into the transformative potential of keto.

Chapter 1

Fueling Your Keto Journey

What is the Ketogenic Diet?

The ketogenic diet, often abbreviated as keto, is a low-carbohydrate, high-fat diet that has gained popularity for its potential benefits in weight loss, improved mental clarity, and enhanced overall well-being. At its core, the ketogenic diet shifts the body's primary source of energy from carbohydrates to fats, inducing a metabolic state known as ketosis. In this state, the body efficiently burns fat for fuel, leading to a reduction in stored body fat.

UNDERSTANDING KETOSIS

Ketosis is a metabolic state where the body utilizes ketones, molecules produced from the breakdown of fats, as an alternative energy source when glucose (sugar) availability is limited. This shift occurs when carbohydrate intake is restricted, typically to about 20-50 grams per day. As a result, the body begins to break down stored fat into ketones, which are then used for energy by the brain and other tissues.

MACRONUTRIENT COMPOSITION

A key aspect of the ketogenic diet is its specific macronutrient composition. The typical macronutrient breakdown for a standard ketogenic diet is:

- High Fat (70-75%): Healthy fats such as avocados, olive oil, nuts, and seeds are emphasized to provide the majority of daily calories.
- Moderate Protein (20-25%): Protein intake is moderate and should come from sources like meat, fish, eggs, and dairy.
- Low Carbohydrate (5-10%): Carbohydrate intake is restricted to a minimal amount, primarily from non-starchy vegetables. This restriction is crucial for inducing and maintaining ketosis.

HEALTH BENEFITS

The ketogenic diet has been associated with various health benefits:
- Weight Loss: By promoting the use of stored fat for energy, the ketogenic diet can lead to effective weight loss.
- Improved Mental Clarity: Some individuals report increased mental focus and clarity when in ketosis, possibly due to the stable energy supply to the brain.
- Stabilized Blood Sugar Levels: With limited carbohydrate intake, blood sugar levels tend to remain stable, benefitting those with insulin resistance or diabetes.

Getting Started with Keto

SETTING REALISTIC GOALS

When embarking on a ketogenic journey, establishing realistic and achievable goals is paramount. These goals serve as a guiding light, keeping you focused and motivated. Here are key considerations for setting realistic goals:

Consideration	Details
Define Your "Why"	Identify your motivation for adopting keto.
Be Specific and Measurable	Set clear and measurable goals for tracking progress.
Gradual Changes	Implement gradual adjustments for a smoother transition.
Account for Non-Scale Victories	Recognize achievements beyond weight loss.
Adjust as Needed	Be open to modifying goals based on experiences and priorities.

By incorporating these elements into your goal-setting process, you create a foundation for success on your ketogenic journey.

FATS, PROTEINS, AND CARBOHYDRATES

Understanding the role of macronutrients—fats, proteins, and carbohydrates—is fundamental to mastering the ketogenic diet. These nutrients form the basis of your daily caloric intake. Let's explore the macronutrients in detail:

Fats: The Primary Energy Source

HEALTHY FATS TABLE:

Fat Source	Serving Size	Calories	Saturated Fat (g)	Monounsaturated Fat (g)	Polyunsaturated Fat (g)
Avocado	1 medium	234	3.2	15.4	2.9
Olive Oil	1 tbsp	119	1.9	9.9	1.4
Almonds	1 oz	160	1.2	9.4	3.5

PROTEINS: BUILDING AND REPAIRING TISSUES

Protein Sources Table:

Protein Source	Serving Size	Calories	Protein (g)	Fat (g)	Carbohydrates (g)
Chicken Breast	3 oz	165	31	3.6	0
Salmon (wild-caught)	3 oz	177	19	11	0
Eggs	2 large	143	13	10	1

CARBOHYDRATES: RESTRICTING FOR KETOSIS

Low-Carb Vegetables Table:

Vegetable	Serving Size	Calories	Carbohydrates (g)	Fiber (g)	Net Carbs (g)
Broccoli	1 cup	55	11.2	5.1	6.1
Cauliflower	1 cup	25	5.3	2.5	2.8
Spinach	1 cup	7	1.1	0.7	0.4

Understanding the macronutrient composition empowers you to make informed dietary choices on your ketogenic journey. Incorporate these healthy fats, moderate proteins, and limited carbohydrates into your meals to support your goals effectively.

What To Eat and What To Avoid

KETO FOODS TO ENJOY

HIGH FAT / LOW CARB (BASED ON NET CARBS)

MEATS & SEAFOOD
- Beef (ground beef, steak, etc.)
- Chicken
- Crab
- Crawfish
- Duck
- Fish
- Goose
- Lamb
- Lobster
- Mussels
- Octopus
- Pork (pork chops, bacon, etc.)
- Quail
- Sausage (without fillers)
- Scallops
- Shrimp
- Veal
- Venison

NUTS & SEEDS
- Almonds
- Brazil nuts
- Chia seeds
- Flaxseeds
- Hazelnuts
- Macadamia nuts
- Peanuts (in moderation)
- Pecans
- Pine nuts
- Pumpkin seeds
- Sacha inchi seeds
- Sesame seeds
- Walnuts

DAIRY
- Blue cheese dressing
- Burrata cheese
- Cottage cheese
- Cream cheese
- Eggs
- Greek yogurt (full-fat)
- Grilling cheese
- Halloumi cheese
- Heavy (whipping) cream
- Kefalotyri cheese
- Mozzarella cheese
- Provolone cheese
- Queso blanco
- Ranch dressing
- Ricotta cheese
- Unsweetened almond milk
- Unsweetened coconut milk

FRUITS
- Blackberries
- Blueberries
- Cranberries
- Raspberries
- Strawberries

VEGETABLES
- Alfalfa sprouts
- Asparagus
- Avocados
- Bell peppers
- Broccoli
- Cabbage
- Carrots (in moderation)
- Cauliflower
- Celery
- Chicory
- Coconut
- Cucumbers
- Garlic (in moderation)
- Green beans
- Herbs
- Jicama
- Lemons
- Limes
- Mushrooms
- Okra
- Olives
- Onions (in moderation)
- Pickles
- Pumpkin
- Radishes
- Salad greens
- Scallions
- Spaghetti squash (in moderation)
- Tomatoes (in moderation)
- Zucchini

KETO FOODS TO AVOID

LOW FAT / HIGH CARB (BASED ON NET CARBS)

MEATS & MEAT ALTERNATIVES

- Deli meat (some, not all)
- Hot dogs (with fillers)
- Sausage (with fillers)
- Seitan
- Tofu

DAIRY

- Almond milk (sweetened)
- Coconut milk (sweetened)
- Milk
- Soy milk (regular)
- Yogurt (regular)

NUTS & SEEDS

- Cashews
- Chestnuts
- Pistachios

VEGETABLES

- Artichokes
- Beans (all varieties)
- Burdock root
- Butternut squash
- Chickpeas
- Corn
- Edamame
- Eggplant
- Leeks
- Parsnips
- Plantains
- Potatoes
- Sweet potatoes
- Winter squash
- Oranges
- Yams

FRUITS &

- Apples
- Apricots
- Bananas
- Boysenberries
- Cantaloupe
- Cherries
- Currants
- Dates
- Elderberries
- Gooseberries
- Grapes
- Honeydew melon
- Huckleberries
- Kiwifruits
- Taro root
- Turnips
- Mangos
- Peaches
- Peas
- Pineapples
- Plums
- Prunes
- Raisins
- Water chestnuts

KETO COOKING STAPLES

1. Pink Himalayan salt
2. Freshly ground black pepper
3. 3 Ghee (clarified butter, without dairy; buy
4. grass-fed if you can)
5. 4 Olive oil
6. Grass-fed butter

KETO PERISHABLES

Eggs (pasture-raised, if you can)
2 Avocados
3 Bacon (uncured)
Cream cheese (full-fat; or use a dairy-free alterna- tive)
Sour cream (full-fat; or use a dairy-free alternative)
Heavy whipping cream or coconut milk (full-fat; I buy the coconut milk in a can)
Garlic (fresh or pre-minced in a jar)
Meat (grass-fed, if you can)
10 Greens (spinach, kale, or arugula)

Common Keto Mistakes

Navigating the ketogenic journey can be transformative, but like any lifestyle change, it comes with its share of challenges. Understanding and avoiding common keto mistakes is crucial for a successful and sustainable experience. In this exploration, we'll dissect prevalent pitfalls and provide insights to help you stay on course.

Inadequate Electrolyte Intake:
One common mistake individuals make when starting keto is overlooking the importance of electrolytes. As the body adjusts to lower carbohydrate intake, there is a natural loss of water and electrolytes. This can lead to symptoms like fatigue, headaches, and muscle cramps, collectively known as the "keto flu."

Electrolyte	Importance on Keto	Food Sources
Sodium	Maintains fluid balance and supports nerve function.	Table salt, bone broth, pickles.
Potassium	Essential for muscle contractions and heart health.	Avocado, spinach, nuts, salmon.
Magnesium	Supports muscle and nerve function, crucial for energy production.	Leafy greens, nuts, seeds, fish.

Ensuring sufficient intake of these electrolytes can alleviate keto flu symptoms and support overall well-being.

NEGLECTING FIBER INTAKE:

In the pursuit of low-carb living, some individuals may unintentionally neglect fiber-rich foods. Adequate fiber intake is crucial for digestive health and can help mitigate potential constipation, a common concern on keto.

Fiber-Rich Foods	Serving Size	Net Carbs	Fiber	Notable Sources
Avocado	1 medium	2g	13g	Healthy fats and a good fiber source.
Chia Seeds	2 tbsp	1g	10g	Packed with fiber and omega-3s.
Broccoli	1 cup	4g	2.4g	Low in net carbs and high in fiber.

Incorporating these fiber-rich foods can support digestive health without compromising your ketogenic goals.

Overlooking Hidden Carbs:
A common pitfall is underestimating the carb content of certain foods, leading to unintentional overconsumption. While focusing on net carbs (total carbs minus fiber), it's essential to be mindful of hidden sources.

Food Item	Net Carbs per Serving	Hidden Carbs
Sugar-Free Snacks	Varies	Some may contain hidden sugars or high-carb additives.
Sauces and Dressings	Varies	Many store-bought options contain added sugars.
Nuts and Nut Butters	Varies	Consuming large quantities may contribute to carb intake.

Reading labels diligently and opting for whole, unprocessed foods can help minimize the risk of hidden carbs derailing your progress.

FEAR OF HEALTHY FATS:

A misconception on keto is the fear of consuming fats, even the healthy ones. While the diet is high in fat, it's crucial to prioritize sources rich in monounsaturated and polyunsaturated fats.

Healthy Fat Sources	Fat Content per Serving	Notable Benefits
Olive Oil	14g	Rich in heart-healthy monounsaturated fats.
Salmon	11g	Provides omega-3 fatty acids for brain health.
Avocado	21g	Packed with monounsaturated fats and various nutrients.

Embracing these healthy fats supports satiety, nutrient absorption, and overall well-being.

LACK OF PLANNING:

A fundamental mistake is embarking on the ketogenic journey without proper planning. Meal preparation is essential to ensure a well-balanced and satisfying diet.

Planning Tips
Create a weekly meal plan with diverse options.
Batch-cook keto-friendly meals for convenience.
Stock up on keto-approved snacks for on-the-go.

Having a plan in place helps you navigate social situations, avoid impulsive food choices, and stay committed to your keto goals.

In conclusion, the ketogenic diet offers numerous benefits, but success hinges on avoiding common pitfalls. By addressing electrolyte needs, prioritizing fiber-rich foods, staying vigilant about hidden carbs, embracing healthy fats, and planning meals effectively, you can navigate the keto journey with confidence and reap the rewards of this transformative lifestyle.

Chapter 2

4-Week Meal Plan

Week 1

DAY 1:
- Breakfast: Creamy Cheddar Deviled Eggs
- Lunch: Turkey Stew with Salsa Verde
- Snack: Skinny Cocktail Meatballs
- Dinner: Classic Italian Bolognese Sauce

Total for the day:
Calories: 1257 | Fat: 86.9g| Carbs: 19g| Protein: 104.5g

DAY 2:
- Breakfast: Creamy Cheddar Deviled Eggs
- Lunch: Turkey Stew with Salsa Verde
- Snack: Skinny Cocktail Meatballs
- Dinner: Classic Italian Bolognese Sauce

Total for the day:
Calories: 1257 | Fat: 86.9g| Carbs: 19g| Protein: 104.5g

DAY 3:
- Breakfast: Creamy Cheddar Deviled Eggs
- Lunch: Turkey Stew with Salsa Verde
- Snack: Skinny Cocktail Meatballs
- Dinner: Classic Italian Bolognese Sauce

Total for the day:
Calories: 1257 | Fat: 86.9g| Carbs: 19g| Protein: 104.5g

DAY 4:
- Breakfast: Creamy Cheddar Deviled Eggs
- Lunch: Classic Italian Bolognese Sauce
- Snack: Skinny Cocktail Meatballs
- Dinner: Turkey Stew with Salsa Verde

Total for the day:
Calories: 1257 | Fat: 86.9g| Carbs: 19g| Protein: 104.5g

DAY 5:
- Breakfast: Creamy Cheddar Deviled Eggs
- Lunch: Classic Italian Bolognese Sauce
- Snack: Skinny Cocktail Meatballs
- Dinner: Turkey Stew with Salsa Verde

Total for the day:
Calories: 1257 | Fat: 86.9g| Carbs: 19g| Protein: 104.5g

Week 2

DAY 1:
- Breakfast: Fontina Cheese and Chorizo Waffles
- Lunch: Chicken Cauliflower Bake
- Snack: Spicy Roasted Pumpkin Seeds
- Dinner: Lobster Pie

Total for the day:
Calories: 1253 | Fat: 95.3g| Carbs: 18.6g| Protein: 69.1g

DAY 2:
- Breakfast: Fontina Cheese and Chorizo Waffles
- Lunch: Chicken Cauliflower Bake
- Snack: Spicy Roasted Pumpkin Seeds
- Dinner: Lobster Pie

Total for the day:
Calories: 1253 | Fat: 95.3g| Carbs: 18.6g| Protein: 69.1g

DAY 3:
- Breakfast: Fontina Cheese and Chorizo Waffles
- Lunch: Chicken Cauliflower Bake
- Snack: Spicy Roasted Pumpkin Seeds
- Dinner: Lobster Pie

Total for the day:
Calories: 1253 | Fat: 95.3g| Carbs: 18.6g| Protein: 69.1g

DAY 4:
- Breakfast: Fontina Cheese and Chorizo Waffles
- Lunch: Lobster Pie
- Snack: Spicy Roasted Pumpkin Seeds
- Dinner: Chicken Cauliflower Bake

Total for the day:
Calories: 1253 | Fat: 95.3g| Carbs: 18.6g| Protein: 69.1g

DAY 5:
- Breakfast: Fontina Cheese and Chorizo Waffles
- Lunch: Lobster Pie
- Snack: Spicy Roasted Pumpkin Seeds
- Dinner: Chicken Cauliflower Bake

Total for the day:
Calories: 1253 | Fat: 95.3g| Carbs: 18.6g| Protein: 69.1g

Week 3

DAY 1:
- Breakfast: Cream Cheese Pancakes
- Lunch: Mind-Blowing Burgers
- Snack: Chocolate Pistachio Truffles
- Dinner: Herbed Pumpkin

Total for the day:
Calories: 1262 | Fat: 107.4g | Carbs: 18.6g | Protein: 48.8g

DAY 2:
- Breakfast: Cream Cheese Pancakes
- Lunch: Mind-Blowing Burgers
- Snack: Chocolate Pistachio Truffles
- Dinner: Herbed Pumpkin

Total for the day:
Calories: 1262 | Fat: 107.4g | Carbs: 18.6g | Protein: 48.8g

DAY 3:
- Breakfast: Cream Cheese Pancakes
- Lunch: Mind-Blowing Burgers
- Snack: Chocolate Pistachio Truffles
- Dinner: Herbed Pumpkin

Total for the day:
Calories: 1262 | Fat: 107.4g | Carbs: 18.6g | Protein: 48.8g

DAY 4:
- Breakfast: Cream Cheese Pancakes
- Lunch: Herbed Pumpkin
- Snack: Chocolate Pistachio Truffles
- Dinner: Mind-Blowing Burgers

Total for the day:
Calories: 1262 | Fat: 107.4g | Carbs: 18.6g | Protein: 48.8g

DAY 5:
- Breakfast: Chocolate Hemp Smoothie
- Lunch: Herbed Pumpkin
- Snack: Chocolate Pistachio Truffles
- Dinner: Mind-Blowing Burgers

Total for the day:
Calories: 1112 | Fat: 89.4g | Carbs: 12.9g | Protein: 46.8g

Week 4

DAY 1:
- Breakfast: Liver Sausages & Onions
- Lunch: Bombay Sloppy Jolenes
- Snack: No-Bake Cheesecake Truffles
- Dinner: Green Bean Casserole

Total for the day:
Calories: 1297 | Fat: 96.6g | Carbs: 20.9g | Protein: 73.9g

DAY 2:
- Breakfast: Liver Sausages & Onions
- Lunch: Bombay Sloppy Jolenes
- Snack: No-Bake Cheesecake Truffles
- Dinner: Green Bean Casserole

Total for the day:
Calories: 1297 | Fat: 96.6g | Carbs: 20.9g | Protein: 73.9g

DAY 3:
- Breakfast: Liver Sausages & Onions
- Lunch: Bombay Sloppy Jolenes
- Snack: No-Bake Cheesecake Truffles
- Dinner: Green Bean Casserole

Total for the day:
Calories: 1297 | Fat: 96.6g | Carbs: 20.9g | Protein: 73.9g

DAY 4:
- Breakfast: Liver Sausages & Onions
- Lunch: Green Bean Casserole
- Snack: No-Bake Cheesecake Truffles
- Dinner: Bombay Sloppy Jolenes

Total for the day:
Calories: 1297 | Fat: 96.6g | Carbs: 20.9g | Protein: 73.9g

DAY 5:
- Breakfast: Liver Sausages & Onions
- Lunch: Green Bean Casserole
- Snack: No-Bake Cheesecake Truffles
- Dinner: Bombay Sloppy Jolenes

Total for the day:
Calories: 1297 | Fat: 96.6g | Carbs: 20.9g | Protein: 73.9g

Chapter 3

Breakfast

Blackberry-Chia Pudding

Prep time: 10 minutes | Cook time: 5 minutes | Serves 2

- 1 cup unsweetened full-fat coconut milk
- 1 teaspoon liquid stevia 1 teaspoon vanilla extract
- ½ cup blackberries, fresh or frozen (no sugar added if frozen)
- ¼ cup chia seeds

1. In a food processor (or blender), process the coconut milk, stevia, and vanilla until the mixture starts to thicken.
2. Add the blackberries, and process until thoroughly mixed and purple. Fold in the chia seeds.

PER SERVING

Calories: 437 | Total Fat: 38g | Carbs: 23g | Net Carbs: 8g | Fiber: 15g | Protein: 8g

Chocolate Hemp Smoothie

Prep time: 5 minutes | Cook time: 15 minutes | Serves 1

- 1 cup unsweetened vanilla-flavored almond milk
- 2 tablespoons heavy whipping cream
- ¼ teaspoon pure vanilla extract
- ¼ cup unsweetened hemp protein powder
- 2 tablespoons unsweetened cocoa powder
- 2 tablespoons granulated erythritol, or more to taste
- 3 ice cubes

1. Place all of the ingredients in a blender and blend until smooth and creamy.
2. Taste and add more sweetener, if desired. Pour into a 12-ounce glass and serve immediately.

PER SERVING

Calories: 245 | Fat: 17g | Protein: 15g | Carbs: 14g | Fiber: 10g | Net Carbs: 4g

Almond Butter Smoothie

Prep time: 5 minutes | Cook time: 5 minutes | Serves 2

- 1 cup unsweetened full-fat coconut milk
- 1 scoop Perfect Keto Exogenous Ketone Powder in chocolate sea salt
- ½ avocado
- 2 tablespoons almond butter
- ½ cup berries, fresh or frozen (no sugar added if frozen)
- ½ cup ice cubes
- ¼ teaspoon liquid stevia (optional)

1. In a blender, combine the coconut milk, protein powder, avocado, almond butter, berries, ice, and stevia (if using).
2. Blend until thoroughly mixed and frothy.
3. Pour into two glasses and enjoy.

PER SERVING

Calories: 446 | Total Fat: 43g | Carbs: 16g | Net Carbs: 9g | Fiber: 7g | Protein: 7g

Cross-Country Scrambler

Prep time: 5 minutes | Cook time: 28 minutes | Serves 2

- 8 strips bacon (about 8 oz/225 g)
- 1 packed cup spiral-sliced butternut squash (about 5¼ oz/150 g)
- ½ green bell pepper, diced
- 6 large eggs, beaten
- ½ cup (40 g) sliced green onions (green parts only)
- ¼ teaspoon ground black pepper

1. Cook the bacon in a large frying pan over medium heat until crispy, about 15 minutes. Remove the bacon from the pan, leaving the grease in the pan. When the bacon has cooled, crumble it.
2. Add the squash and bell pepper to the pan with the bacon grease. Cover and cook over medium-low heat for 8 minutes, or until the vegetables are fork-tender.
3. Add the beaten eggs, green onions, and black pepper. Mix with a large spoon until fully incorporated.
4. Cook, uncovered, for 5 minutes, stirring every minute, or until the eggs are cooked to your liking. Once complete, fold in half of the crumbled bacon.
5. Divide evenly between 2 plates, top with remaining crumbled bacon, and dig in!

PER SERVING

Calories: 395 | Fat: 27 g | Carbs: 11.7 g | Dietary Fiber: 2.5 g | Net Carbs: 9.2 g | Sugars: 1.8 g | Protein: 26.3 g

Creamy Coconut Porridge

Prep time: 5 minutes | Cook time: 15 minutes | Serves 2

- 4 tablespoons coconut flour
- 2 tablespoons flaxseed meal
- 1 tablespoon pumpkin seeds, ground
- 2 tablespoons pecans, ground
- 1/4 teaspoon ground cinnamon
- 1/2 teaspoon vanilla paste
- 1/2 cup canned coconut milk
- 1/2 cup water
- 4 tablespoons double cream
- 4 tablespoons xylitol

1. Mix the ingredients in a sauté pan over moderate heat.
2. Now, simmer the mixture for about 8 minutes or until thoroughly heated.
3. Divide your porridge between two serving bowls and serve warm. Devour!

PER SERVING

Calories: 300 | Fat: 25.1g | Carbs: 8g | Protein: 4.9g | Fiber: 6g

Pineapple Ginger Smoothie

Prep time: 8 minutes | Cook time: 15 minutes | Serves 1

- 1 cup unsweetened vanilla-flavored almond milk
- ¼ cup chopped fresh pineapple
- 2 tablespoons collagen powder
- 1 tablespoon granulated erythritol, or more to taste
- 2 teaspoons chopped fresh turmeric, or 1 teaspoon turmeric powder
- 1 teaspoon peeled and minced fresh ginger
- 3 ice cubes

1. Place all of the ingredients in a blender and blend until smooth and creamy.
2. Taste and add more sweetener, if desired. Pour into a 12-ounce glass and serve immediately.

PER SERVING

Calories: 149 | Fat: 7g | Protein: 12g | Carbs: 9g | Fiber: 2g | Net Carbs: 7g

Liver Sausages & Onions

Prep time: 10 minutes | **Cook time:** 26 minutes | **Serves** 6

Sausages:

- 8 ounces (225 g) chicken livers
- 1 tablespoon apple cider vinegar
- 1 pound (455 g) ground beef
- 1 pound (455 g) ground pork
- 2½ teaspoons dried rubbed sage
- 1¼ teaspoons dried rosemary leaves
- 1 teaspoon dried thyme leaves
- 1 teaspoon finely ground sea salt
- ¾ teaspoon ground black pepper
- 4 cloves garlic, minced
- ¼ cup (60 ml) avocado oil, or ¼ cup (55 g) coconut oil or ghee, for the pan
- 2 medium-sized white onions, thinly sliced

1. Place the chicken livers in a medium-sized bowl and cover with water. Add the vinegar. Cover and place in the fridge to soak for 24 to 48 hours.
2. Rinse and drain the livers, then place them in a blender or food processor. Blend until smooth.
3. Transfer the pureed livers to a large mixing bowl and add the remaining ingredients for the sausages. Mix thoroughly with your hands to combine.
4. Heat the oil in a large frying pan over medium-low heat.
5. While the oil is heating, form the liver mixture into patties: Using a ¼-cup (60-ml) scoop, scoop up portions of the mixture and roll between your hands to form into 12 balls about 1¾ inches (4.5 cm) in diameter. Place the balls in the hot pan and press down until they're ½ inch (1.25 cm) thick. Do not overcrowd the pan; you may have to cook the sausages in two batches if they don't all fit comfortably.
6. Cook the sausages for 8 minutes per side, or until no longer pink in the center.
7. Place the cooked sausages on a serving plate. Set in a 180°F (82°C) oven to keep warm, if you wish.
8. Once the sausages are done, place the sliced onions in the same pan and cook for 10 minutes, or until translucent, stirring every minute or so.
9. Transfer the cooked onions to the serving plate with the sausages and enjoy.

PER SERVING

Calories: 392 | Fat: 21.9 g | Carbs: 5.6 g | Dietary Fiber: 1.6 g | Net Carbs: 4 g | Sugars: 1.6 g | Protein: 43.2 g

Creamy Cheddar Deviled Eggs

Prep time: 20 minutes | **Cook time:** 10 minutes | **Serves** 5

- 10 eggs
- ¼ cup mayonnaise
- tbsp tomato paste
- tbsp celery, chopped
- 2 tbsp carrot, chopped
- 2 tbsp chives, minced
- 2 tbsp cheddar cheese, grated
- Salt and black pepper, to taste

1. Place the eggs in a pot and fill with water by about 1 inch. Bring the eggs to a boil over high heat, then reduce the heat to medium and simmer for 10 minutes.
2. Remove and rinse under running water until cooled. Peel and discard the shell. Slice each egg in half lengthwise and get rid of the yolks. Mix the yolks with the rest of the ingredients. Split the mixture amongst the egg whites and set deviled eggs on a plate to serve.

PER SERVING

Calories: 177 | Fat: 12.7g | Net Carbs: 4.6g | Protein: 11.4g

Mushroom & Cheese Lettuce Wraps

Prep time: 20 minutes | Cook time: 9 minutes | Serves 4

For The Wraps:
- 6 eggs
- 2 tbsp almond milk
- 1 tbsp olive oil
- Sea salt, to taste

For The Filling:
- 1 tsp olive oil
- 1 cup mushrooms, chopped
- Salt and black pepper, to taste
- ½ tsp cayenne pepper
- 8 fresh lettuce leaves
- 4 slices gruyere cheese
- 2 tomatoes, sliced

1. Mix all the ingredients for the wraps thoroughly.
2. Set a frying pan over medium heat. Add in ¼ of the mixture and cook for 4 minutes on both sides. Do the same thrice and set the wraps aside, they should be kept warm.
3. In a separate pan over medium heat, warm 1 teaspoon of olive oil. Cook the mushrooms for 5 minutes until soft; add cayenne pepper, black pepper, and salt. Set 1-2 lettuce leaves onto every wrap, split the mushrooms among the wraps and top with tomatoes and cheese.

PER SERVING

Calories: 472 | Fat: 44g | Net Carbs: 5.4g | Protein: 19.5g

Bacon & Cheese Pesto Mug Cakes

Prep time: 8 minutes | Cook time: 5 minutes | Serves 2

- ¼ cup flax meal
- 1 egg
- 2 tbsp heavy cream 2 tbsp pesto
- ¼ cup almond flour
- ¼ tsp baking soda
- Salt and black pepper, to taste
- Filling:
- 2 tbsp cream cheese
- 4 slices bacon
- ½ medium avocado, sliced

1. Mix together the dry muffin ingredients in a bowl. Add egg, heavy cream, and pesto, and whisk well with a fork. Season with salt and pepper. Divide the mixture between two ramekins.
2. Place in the microwave and cook for 60-90 seconds. Leave to cool slightly before filling.
3. Meanwhile, in a skillet, over medium heat, cook the bacon slices until crispy. Transfer to paper towels to soak up excess fat; set aside. Invert the muffins onto a plate and cut in half, crosswise. To assemble the sandwiches: spread cream cheese and top with bacon and avocado slices.

PER SERVING

Calories: 511 | Fat: 38.2g | Net Carbs: 4.5g | Protein: 16.4g

The XXL Keto Diet Cookbook

Grain-Free Hemp Seed Porridge

Prep time: 2 minutes | Cook time: 3 minutes | Serves 2

Porridge
- 1 cup (240 ml) nondairy milk
- ½ cup (75 g) hulled hemp seeds
- 2 tablespoons roughly ground flax seeds
- 2 tablespoons coconut oil
- 1 tablespoon chia seeds
- 1 tablespoon confectioners'-style erythritol or granulated xylitol or 5 drops liquid stevia
- ¾ teaspoon vanilla extract
- ¾ teaspoon ground cinnamon
- ¼ cup (28 g) almond meal or blanched almond flour (see note, above)

Toppings
- 4 raw Brazil nuts or small handful of nuts of choice, roughly chopped
- 2 tablespoons hulled hemp seeds
- Fresh berries (optional)
- Additional nondairy milk, for serving (optional)

1. Put all the ingredients for the porridge, except the almond meal, in a small saucepan. Stir to combine, then bring to a gentle boil over medium heat.
2. Once bubbling lightly, stir, then cover and cook for 1 to 2 minutes.
3. Remove from the heat, stir in the almond meal, and divide between 2 serving bowls. Divide the toppings evenly between the bowls and eat immediately with a splash of nondairy milk, if desired.

PER SERVING

Calories: 660 | Fat: 55.7g | Saturated Fat: 17.1g | Carbs: 15.2g | Dietary Fiber: 12.5g | Net Carbs: 2.7g | Sugars: 1.1g | Protein: 24.5g

Almond Waffles with Cinnamon Cream

Prep time: 25 minutes | Cook time: 15 minutes | Serves 6

- For The Spread
- 8 oz cream cheese, at room temperature
- 1 tsp cinnamon powder
- 3 tbsp swerve brown sugar
- Cinnamon powder for garnishing
- For The Waffles
- 5 tbsp melted butter
- 1 ½ cups unsweetened almond milk
- 7 large eggs
- ¼ tsp liquid stevia
- ½ tsp baking powder
- 1 ½ cups almond flour

1. Combine the cream cheese, cinnamon, and swerve with a hand mixer until smooth. Cover and chill until ready to use.
2. To make the waffles, whisk the butter, milk, and eggs in a medium bowl. Add the stevia and baking powder and mix. Stir in the almond flour and combine until no lumps exist. Let the batter sit for 5 minutes to thicken. Spritz a waffle iron with a non-stick cooking spray. Ladle a ¼ cup of the batter into the waffle iron and cook according to the manufacturer's instructions until golden, about 10 minutes in total. Repeat with the remaining batter.
3. Slice the waffles into quarters; apply the cinnamon spread in between each of two waffles and snap. Sprinkle with cinnamon powder and serve.

PER SERVING

Calories: 307 | Fat: 24g | Net Carbs: 8g | Protein: 12g

Spicy Breakfast Scramble

Prep time: 5 minutes | Cook time: 10 minutes | Serves 2

- 2 tablespoons ghee
- 6 ounces Mexican chorizo or other spicy sausage
- 6 large eggs
- 2 tablespoons heavy (whipping) cream
- Pink Himalayan salt
- ½ cup chopped scallions, white and green parts

1. In a large skillet over medium-high heat, melt the ghee. Add the sausage and sauté, browning for about 6 minutes, until cooked through.
2. In a medium bowl, whisk the eggs until frothy.
3. Add the cream, and season with pink Himalayan salt and pepper. Whisk to blend thoroughly.
4. Leaving the fat in the skillet, push the sausage to one side. Add the egg mixture to the other side of the skillet and heat until almost cooked through, about 3 minutes.
5. When the eggs are almost done, mix in half of the shredded cheese.
6. Spoon onto two plates and serve hot.

PER SERVING

Calories: 850 | Total Fat: 70g | Carbs: 7g | Net Carbs: 6g | Fiber: 1g | Protein: 46g

Fontina Cheese and Chorizo Waffles

Prep time: 30 minutes | Cook time: 5 minutes | Serves 6

- 6 eggs
- 6 tbsp almond milk
- 1 tsp Spanish spice mix or allspice
- Sea salt and black pepper, to taste
- 3 chorizo sausages, cooked, chopped
- 1 cup fontina cheese, shredded

1. Using a mixing bowl, beat the eggs, Spanish spice mix, black pepper, salt, and almond milk. Add in shredded cheese and chopped sausage. Use a nonstick cooking spray to spray a waffle iron.
2. Cook the egg mixture for 5 minutes. Serve alongside homemade sugar-free tomato ketchup.

PER SERVING

Calories: 316 | Fat: 25g | Net Carbs: 1.5g | Protein: 20.2g

Cream Cheese Pancakes

Prep time: 5 minutes | Cook time: 12 minutes | Makes 4 (6-inch) pancakes

- 2 ounces cream cheese (¼ cup), softened
- 2 large eggs
- 1 teaspoon granulated erythritol
- ½ teaspoon ground cinnamon
- 1 tablespoon butter, for the pan

1. Place the cream cheese, eggs, sweetener, and cinnamon in a small blender and blend for 30 seconds, or until smooth. Let the batter rest for 2 minutes.
2. Heat the butter in a 10-inch nonstick skillet over medium heat until bubbling. Pour ¼ cup of the batter into the pan and tilt the pan in a circular motion to create a thin pancake about 6 inches in diameter. Cook for 2 minutes, or until the center is no longer glossy. Flip and cook for 1 minute on the other side. Remove and repeat with the rest of the batter, making a total of 4 pancakes.

PER SERVING

Calories: 395 | Fat: 35g | Protein: 17g | Carbs: 3g | Fiber: 0g | Net Carbs: 3g

Early-Day Jambalaya

Prep time: 25 minutes | **Cook time:** 25 minutes | Serves 4

- ⅓ cup (69 g) lard
- 4 sausages (about 8 ounces/225 g), cooked and chopped
- 1 cup (180 g) cubed cooked skinless chicken thighs
- 1¼ cups (210 g) diced celery
- ½ packed cup chopped green onions
- 2 tablespoons Cajun Seasoning
- 2½ cups (400 g) riced cauliflower florets
- ½ cup (120 ml) chicken bone broth
- ¼ cup (50 g) diced tomatoes
- Handful of chopped fresh parsley (optional)

1. Melt the lard in a large frying pan over medium heat, then add the chopped sausages, cubed chicken thighs, celery, green onions, and Cajun seasoning. Cook for 10 minutes, or until the celery has softened.
2. Add the cauliflower and bone broth. Cover and cook for 5 minutes, or until the cauliflower is fork-tender.
3. Stir in the diced tomatoes and increase the heat to high. Cook, uncovered, for 5 to 7 minutes, until most of the liquid has evaporated.
4. Remove from the heat, toss in a handful of chopped fresh parsley, if desired, and divide among 4 small serving bowls.

PER SERVING

Calories: 458 | Fat: 37.6g | Saturated Fat: 13.2g || Carbs: 7.6g | Dietary Fiber: 3.5g | Net Carbs: 4.1g | Sugars: 3.4g | Protein: 22.4g

Keto Breakfast Pudding

Prep time: 5 minutes | **Cook time:** 5 minutes | Serves 3

- 1½ cups (350 ml) full-fat coconut milk
- 1 cup (110 g) frozen raspberries
- ¼ cup (60 ml) MCT oil or melted coconut oil, or ¼ cup (40 g) unflavored MCT oil powder
- ¼ cup (40 g) collagen peptides or protein powder
- 2 tablespoons chia seeds
- 1 tablespoon apple cider vinegar
- 1 teaspoon vanilla extract
- 1 tablespoon erythritol, or 4 drops liquid stevia

Toppings (Optional):
- Unsweetened shredded coconut
- Hulled hemp seeds
- Fresh berries of choice

1. Place all the pudding ingredients in a blender or food processor and blend until smooth.
2. Serve in bowls with your favorite toppings, if desired.

PER SERVING

Calories: 403 | Fat: 34.2 g | Saturated Fat: 30.8 g | Carbs: 8.8 g | Dietary Fiber: 3.1 g | Net Carbs: 5.7 g | Sugars: 3.4 g | Protein: 15.2 g

Spicy Eggs with Turkey Ham

Prep time: 15 minutes | Cook time: 11 minutes | Serves 2

- 2 tbsp olive oil
- ½ cup onion, chopped
- 1 tsp smashed garlic
- 1 tsp serrano pepper, deveined and minced
- Salt and black pepper to taste
- 5 ounces turkey ham, chopped
- 4 eggs, whisked
- 1 thyme sprig, chopped
- ½ cup olives, pitted and sliced

1. Over medium heat, set a skillet and warm oil; add in onion and sauté for 4 minutes until tender. Stir in garlic, salt, ham, black pepper, and serrano pepper; cook for 5-6 more minutes.
2. Add in eggs and sprinkle with thyme; cook for 5 minutes. Garnish with sliced olives before serving.

PER SERVING

Calories: 462 | Fat: 40.6g | Net Carbs: 7.1g | Protein: 16.9g

Ginger & Walnut Porridge

Prep time: 25 minutes | Cook time: 5 minutes | Serves 2

- 1 eggs
- 2 tbsp swerve
- ½ cup heavy cream
- 1 ½ tbsp coconut oil
- ½ tsp ginger paste
- ¼ tsp turmeric powder
- ¼ cup walnuts, chopped

1. In a bowl, mix swerve, eggs and heavy cream. Set a pot over medium heat and warm coconut oil. Add in egg/cream mixture and cook until cooked through. Kill the heat and place in turmeric and ginger paste.
2. Split the porridge into bowls, top with chopped walnuts and serve.

PER SERVING

Calories: 430 | Fat: 41.1g | Net Carbs: 9.8g | Protein: 11.4g

Indian Masala Omelet

Prep time: 8 minutes | Cook time: 25 minutes | Serves 2

- 3 tablespoons avocado oil, coconut oil, or ghee
- ¼ cup (20 g) sliced green onions
- 1 clove garlic, minced
- 1 small tomato, diced
- 1½ teaspoons curry powder
- ½ teaspoon garam masala
- 6 large eggs, beaten
- ¼ cup (15 g) chopped fresh cilantro leaves and stems

1. Heat the oil in a large frying pan over medium heat until it shimmers. When the oil is shimmering, add the green onions, garlic, tomato, and chili pepper. Cook for 10 minutes, or until the liquid from the tomatoes has evaporated.
2. Reduce the heat to low and sprinkle the tomato mixture with the curry powder and garam masala. Stir to incorporate, then drizzle the beaten eggs over the top.
3. Cover and cook for 5 minutes, or until the edges are cooked through.
4. Sprinkle with the cilantro, fold one side over the other, cover, and cook for another 10 minutes.

PER SERVING

Calories: 438 | Fat: 36.3 g | Carbs: 7.7 g | Dietary Fiber: 1.9 g | Net Carbs: 5.8 g | Sugars: 4.2 g | Protein: 20.2 g

Sausage Breakfast Stacks

Prep time: 10 minutes | Cook time: 15 minutes | Serves 2

- 8 ounces ground pork
- ½ teaspoon garlic powder
- ½ teaspoon onion powder
- 2 tablespoons ghee, divided
- 2 large eggs
- 1 avocado
- Pink Himalayan salt
- Freshly ground black pepper

1. Preheat the oven to 375°F.
2. In a medium bowl, mix well to combine the ground pork, garlic powder, and onion powder. Form the mixture into 2 patties.
3. In a medium skillet over medium-high heat, melt 1 tablespoon of ghee.
4. Add the sausage patties and cook for 2 minutes on each side, until browned.
5. Transfer the sausage to a baking sheet. Cook in the oven for 8 to 10 minutes, until cooked through.
6. Add the remaining 1 tablespoon of ghee to the skillet. When it is hot, crack the eggs into the skillet and cook without disturbing for about 3 minutes, until the whites are opaque and the yolks have set.
7. Meanwhile, in a small bowl, mash the avocado.
8. Season the eggs with pink Himalayan salt and pepper.
9. Remove the cooked sausage patties from the oven.
10. Place a sausage patty on each of two warmed plates. Spread half of the mashed avocado on top of each sausage patty, and top each with a fried egg. Serve hot.

PER SERVING

Calories: 533 | Total Fat: 44g | Carbs: 7g | Net Carbs: 3g | Fiber: 5g | Protein: 29g

Sausage and Greens Hash Bowl

Prep time: 25 minutes | Cook time: 25 minutes | Serves 2

Hash
- ⅔ cup (100 g) peeled and ½-inch-cubed rutabaga
- 2 tablespoons lard
- 2 precooked sausages (about 4 ounces/115 g), cut into ½-inch cubes
- ¼ cup (20 g) chopped green onions, green parts only

For The Bowls
- 2 cups (140 g) fresh spinach
- ½ large Hass avocado, sliced
- 2 strips bacon, cooked and cut into bite-sized pieces
- 1 teaspoon finely chopped fresh parsley

1. Steam the rutabaga for 8 to 10 minutes, until fork-tender.
2. Melt the lard in a medium-sized frying pan over medium heat. Add the steamed rutabaga and cook for 7 to 10 minutes, until the rutabaga begins to brown.
3. Add the sausages and green onions and cook for 3 to 5 minutes, until the sausages begin to brown.
4. Meanwhile, assemble the bowls: Divide the spinach equally between 2 medium-sized serving bowls. When the hash is ready, divide it equally between the bowls, laying it on top of the bed of spinach. Place equal amounts of the sliced avocado, bacon pieces, and parsley on top.

PER SERVING

Calories: 560 | Fat: 49.7g | Carbs: 11.6g | Dietary Fiber: 6g | Net Carbs: 5.6g | Sugars: 3.6g | Protein: 16.6g

Grilled Halloumi Cheese with Eggs

Prep time: 20 minutes | Cook time: 15 minutes | Serves 4

- 4 slices halloumi cheese
- 2 tbsp olive oil
- 1 tsp dried Greek seasoning blend
- 6 eggs, beaten
- ½ tsp sea salt
- ¼ tsp crushed red pepper flakes
- 1 ½ cups avocado, pitted and sliced
- 1 cup grape tomatoes, halved
- 4 tbsp pecans, chopped

1. Preheat your grill to medium. Set the halloumi in the center of a piece of heavy-duty foil. Sprinkle oil over the halloumi and apply Greek seasoning blend. Close the foil to create a packet. Grill for about 15 minutes; then slice into four pieces.
2. In a frying pan, warm the olive oil and cook the eggs. Stir well to create large and soft curds. Season with salt and red pepper flakes. Put the eggs and grilled cheese on a serving bowl. Serve alongside tomatoes and avocado, decorated with chopped pecans.

PER SERVING

Calories: 542 | Fat: 46.4g | Net Carbs: 11.2g | Protein: 23.7g

Coconut Chai Vanilla Smoothie

Prep time: 5 minutes | Cook time: 15 minutes | Serves 1

- ½ cup brewed chai tea, cooled
- ½ cup unsweetened vanilla-flavored almond milk
- 2 tablespoons full-fat unsweetened coconut milk
- 2 tablespoons sugar-free vanilla-flavored protein powder
- 1 tablespoon granulated erythritol, or more to taste
- ¼ teaspoon pure vanilla extract
- ⅛ teaspoon ground cinnamon, plus more for garnish if desired
- 3 ice cubes

1. Place all of the ingredients in a blender and blend until smooth and creamy.
2. Taste and add more sweetener, if desired. Pour into a 12-ounce glass and serve immediately. Garnish with a dusting of cinnamon, if desired.

PER SERVING

Calories: 170 | Fat: 8g | Protein: 18g | Carbs: 4g | Fiber: 1g | Net Carbs: 3g

Bacon Lovers' Quiche

Prep time: 20 minutes | Cook time: 45 minutes | Serves 8

Crust
- 2 cups (220 g) blanched almond flour
- 1 large egg
- 2 tablespoons melted lard, plus more for the pans
- ⅛ teaspoon finely ground gray sea salt

Filling
- 6 strips bacon (about 6 ounces/170 g)
- 1⅓ cups (315 ml) full-fat coconut milk
- 4 large eggs
- ¼ cup plus 2 tablespoons (25 g) nutritional yeast
- ¼ teaspoon finely ground gray sea salt
- ¼ teaspoon ground black pepper
- ⅛ teaspoon ground nutmeg

For Garnish (optional)
- Cooked chopped bacon (reserved from above)
- Sliced fresh chives

1. Preheat the oven to 350°F (177°C) and lightly grease four 4-inch (10-cm) tart pans with lard.
2. Make the crusts: In a large bowl, combine the almond flour, egg, lard, and salt. Mix with a fork until completely incorporated.
3. Divide the dough into 4 pieces and place each piece in a prepared tart pan. Press the dough into the pans, pushing it evenly up the sides. It should be about ⅛ inch (3 mm) thick.
4. Place the tart pans on a rimmed baking sheet and par-bake for 13 to 15 minutes, until the crusts are lightly golden.
5. Meanwhile, prepare the filling: Cook the bacon in a frying pan over medium heat until crispy, then roughly chop or crumble it; reserve the bacon grease. Put the coconut milk, eggs, nutritional yeast, salt, pepper, and nutmeg in a bowl. Add the bacon pieces (setting a small amount aside for garnish if you wish) and still-warm reserved bacon grease and whisk to combine.
6. Remove the par-baked crusts from the oven and reduce the temperature to 325°F (163°C). Leaving the crusts on the baking sheet, fill them all the way to the brim with the egg filling.
7. Return the quiches to the oven and bake for 30 minutes, or until the tops are lightly golden. Allow to cool for 30 minutes before serving. Garnish each quiche with the reserved bacon pieces and/or sliced chives, if desired.

PER ½ QUICHE

Calories: 404 | Fat: 30.7g | Carbs: 9g | Dietary Fiber: 5g | Net Carbs: 4g | Sugars: 1.2g | Protein: 22.9g

Double-Pork Frittata

Prep time: 5 minutes | Cook time: 25 minutes | Serves 4

- 1 tablespoon butter or pork lard
- 8 large eggs
- 1 cup heavy (whipping) cream
- Pink Himalayan salt
- Freshly ground black pepper
- 4 ounces pancetta, chopped
- 2 ounces prosciutto, thinly sliced
- 1 tablespoon chopped fresh dill

1. Preheat the oven to 375°F. Coat a 9-by-13-inch baking pan with the butter.
2. In a large bowl, whisk the eggs and cream together. Season with pink Himalayan salt and pepper, and whisk to blend.
3. Pour the egg mixture into the prepared pan. Sprinkle the pancetta in and distribute evenly throughout.
4. Tear off pieces of the prosciutto and place on top, then sprinkle with the dill.
5. Bake for about 25 minutes, or until the edges are golden and the eggs are just set.
6. Transfer to a rack to cool for 5 minutes.
7. Cut into 4 portions and serve hot.

PER SERVING

Calories: 437 | Total Fat: 39g | Carbs: 3g | Net Carbs: 3g | Fiber: 0g | Protein: 21g

Eggs Benedict

Prep time: 10 minutes | Cook time:16 minutes |Serves 4

- 2 Mug Biscuits
- 2 teaspoons apple cider vinegar
- 4 large eggs
- 4 slices Canadian bacon
- ½ cup (120 ml) Ready-in-Seconds Hollandaise Sauce
- 2 tablespoons finely chopped fresh parsley, for garnish

1. Cut the biscuits in half and set each half on a separate plate.
2. Fill a large saucepan two-thirds full with water and bring to a light simmer over medium-low heat. Once simmering, add the vinegar.
3. Crack each egg into a separate small bowl, then gently slide an egg into the lightly simmering water. Once the egg begins to turn white, add another egg, and so on until all the eggs are in the saucepan. Cook for 2 minutes, then turn off the heat and allow the eggs to sit in the hot water bath for 8 minutes before removing with a slotted spoon.
4. Meanwhile, place the Canadian bacon in a large frying pan and fry over medium heat for 3 minutes per side, or until lightly golden.
5. Top each biscuit half with a slice of the pan-fried Canadian bacon and a poached egg, finishing each with 2 tablespoons of hollandaise sauce.
6. Sprinkle with the parsley and enjoy immediately.

PER SERVING

Calories: 399 | Fat: 38.2 g | Carbs: 5.7 g | Dietary Fiber: 2.8 g | Net Carbs: 2.9 g | Sugars: 1 g | Protein: 8.1 g

Chimichurri Steak Bunwiches

Prep time: 10 minutes | Cook time: 5 minutes | Serves 1

- 8 large eggs
- ½ teaspoon garlic powder
- ½ teaspoon onion powder
- ¼ teaspoon finely ground sea salt
- ¼ teaspoon ground black pepper
- 2 tablespoons avocado oil
- 1 cup (212 g) Chimichurri, divided
- 1 pound (455 g) skirt steak or flank steak, grilled and thinly sliced
- 4 cups (113 g) mixed greens
- Special Equipment
- 8 mason jar lid rings without the tops

1. Crack the eggs into a medium-sized bowl. Add the garlic powder, onion powder, salt, and pepper and whisk until just combined.
2. Drizzle the oil into a large frying pan. Before heating, use your fingers to oil the insides of the lid rings. Place the oiled rings flat side down in the pan and turn the heat to medium-low. Allow the pan to heat up for 1 minute before dividing the egg mixture among the rings, pouring about ¼ cup (60 ml) into each ring, or until the egg mixture just reaches the rim.
3. Cover and cook for 5 minutes, or until the eggs are cooked through. Remove from the heat and let sit for 2 minutes, then use a spatula to remove the lid rings and cooked eggs from the pan. Carefully remove the egg buns from the rings.
4. To assemble the bunwiches, spoon 2 tablespoons of the chimichurri onto an egg bun, then place one-quarter of the steak on the chimichurri. Take a second egg bun and place it on top of the steak. Repeat to make a total of 4 sandwiches.
5. Serve each bunwich with 1 cup of the greens, and top each portion of greens with 2 tablespoons of chimichurri. Enjoy!

PER SERVING

Calories: 593 | Fat: 43 g | Carbs: 6.2 g | Dietary Fiber: 1.9 g | Net Carbs: 4.3 g | Sugars: 2.1 g | Protein: 45.3 g

Cacao Coconut Granola

Prep time: 5 minutes | Cook time: 30 minutes | Makes 3 cups

- ½ cup chopped raw pecans
- ½ cup flax seeds
- ½ cup superfine blanched almond flour
- ½ cup unsweetened dried coconut
- ¼ cup chopped cacao nibs
- ¼ cup chopped raw walnuts
- 3 tablespoons granulated erythritol
- 1 teaspoon ground cinnamon
- ⅛ teaspoon kosher salt
- ⅓ cup coconut oil
- 1 large egg white, beaten

1. Preheat the oven to 300°F. Line a 15 by 10-inch sheet pan with parchment paper.
2. Place all of the ingredients in a large bowl. Stir well until the mixture is crumbly and holds together in small clumps. Spread out on the parchment-lined pan. Bake for 30 minutes, or until golden brown and fragrant.
3. Let the granola cool completely in the pan before removing. Store in an airtight container in the refrigerator for up to 2 weeks.

PER SERVING

Calories: 441 | Fat: 40g | Protein: 15g | Carbs: 14g | Fiber: 10g | Net Carbs: 4g

Pepper Sausage Fry

Prep time: 5 minutes | Cook time: 20 minutes | Serves 4

- ¼ cup (60 ml) avocado oil, or ¼ cup (55 g) coconut oil
- 12 ounces (340 g) smoked sausages, thinly sliced
- 1 small green bell pepper, thinly sliced
- 1 small red bell pepper, thinly sliced
- 1½ teaspoons garlic powder
- 1 teaspoon dried oregano leaves
- 1 teaspoon paprika
- ¼ teaspoon finely ground sea salt
- ¼ teaspoon ground black pepper
- ¼ cup (17 g) chopped fresh parsley

1. Heat the oil in a large frying pan over medium-low heat until it shimmers.
2. When the oil is shimmering, add the rest of the ingredients, except the parsley. Cover and cook for 15 minutes, until the bell peppers are fork-tender.
3. Remove the lid and continue to cook for 5 to 6 minutes, until the liquid evaporates.
4. Remove from the heat, stir in the parsley, and serve.

PER SERVING

Calories: 411 | Fat: 38.3 g | Carbs: 6.3 g | Dietary Fiber: 1.5 g | Net Carbs: 4.8 g | Sugars: 1.9 g | Protein: 11.1 g

Crêpes with Lemon-Buttery Syrup

Prep time: 25 minutes | Cook time: 8 minutes | Serves 6

Crêpes:
- 6 ounces mascarpone cheese, softened
- 6 eggs
- ½ tbsp granulated swerve
- ¼ cup almond flour 1 tsp baking soda 1 tsp baking powder

Syrup:
- ¾ cup water
- tbsp lemon juice
- 1 tbsp butter
- ¾ cup swerve, powdered
- 1 tbsp vanilla extract
- ½ tsp xanthan gum

1. with the use of an electric mixer, mix all crepes ingredients until well incorporated.
2. Use melted butter to grease a frying pan and set over medium heat; cook the crepes until the edges start to brown, about 2 minutes. Flip over and cook the other side for a further 2 minutes; repeat the process with the remaining batter. Put the crepes on a plate.
3. In the same pan, mix swerve, butter and water; simmer for 6 minutes as you stir. Transfer the mixture to a blender together with a ¼ teaspoon of xanthan gum and vanilla extract and mix well. Place in the remaining xanthan gum, lemon juice, and allow to sit until the syrup is thick.

PER SERVING

Calories: 243 | Fat: 19.6g | Net Carbs: 5.5g | Protein: 11g

The XXL Keto Diet Cookbook

Chapter 4

Snacks and Appetizers

Coconut Flour Cheese Crackers

Prep time: 25 minutes | Cook time: 20 minutes |Serves 4

- 1 cup coconut flour
- 1 cup fontina cheese, grated
- Salt and black pepper to taste
- ¼ tsp garlic powder
- ¼ tsp onion powder
- ¼ cup butter, softened
- ¼ tsp smoked paprika
- ¼ cup heavy cream

1. Preheat the oven to 350 F.
2. Mix the coconut flour, fontina cheese, salt, pepper, garlic powder, onion powder, and smoked paprika in a bowl. Add in the butter and mix well. Top with the heavy cream and mix again until smooth, add 1 to 2 tablespoon of water, if it is too thick.
3. Place the dough on a cutting board and cover with plastic wrap. Use a rolling pin to spread out the dough into a light rectangle. Cut cracker squares out of the dough and arrange them on a baking sheet without overlapping. Bake for 20 minutes until browned. Let cool completely before serving.

PER SERVING

Calories: 287 | Fat: 26.3g | Net Carbs: 3.1g | Protein 10.5g

Skinny Cocktail Meatballs

Prep time: 5 minutes | Cook time:15 minutes |Serves 6

- ¼ pound ground turkey
- ¼ pound ground pork
- 1 ounce bacon, chopped
- ¼ cup flaxseed meal
- 1/2 teaspoon garlic, pressed
- 1 egg, beaten
- 1/2 cup cheddar cheese, shredded Sea salt, to season
- 1/4 teaspoon ground black pepper
- 1/4 teaspoon cayenne pepper
- 1/4 teaspoon marjoram

1. Start by preheating your oven to 395 degrees F.
2. Thoroughly combine all ingredients in a mixing bowl. Now, form the mixture into meatballs.
3. Place your meatballs in a parchment-lined baking sheet. Bake in the preheated oven for about 18 minutes, rotating the pan halfway through.
4. Serve with toothpicks and enjoy!

PER SERVING

Calories: 569 | Fat: 42.2g | Carbs: 6.5g | Protein: 40.1g | Fiber: 5.7g

Radish Chips & Cheese Bites

Prep time: 15 minutes | Cook time: 10 minutes |Serves 4

- ½ cup cheddar cheese, shredded
- ¼ cup natural yogurt
- ½ cup pecorino cheese, grated
- 1 tbsp tomato puree
- ½ tsp dried rosemary, crushed
- ¼ tsp dried thyme leaves, crushed
- Salt and black pepper, to taste
- 1 pound radishes, sliced
- 1 tbsp olive oil

1. Preheat oven to 400 F. Coat radishes with salt, pepper and olive oil. Arrange in a single layer on a cookie sheet. Bake for 10 minutes, shaking once or twice.
2. In a mixing bowl, mix cheddar cheese, tomato puree, black pepper, salt, rosemary, yogurt, and thyme. Place in foil liners-candy cups and serve with the radish chips.

PER SERVING

Calories: 167 | Fat 13.2g | Net Carbs: 5.3g | Protein 9.1g

Baked Zucchini Gratin

Prep time: 10 minutes| Cook time: 25 minutes| Serves 2

- 1 large zucchini, cut into ¼-inch-thick slices
- Pink Himalayan salt
- 1 ounce Brie cheese, rind trimmed off
- 1 tablespoon butter
- Freshly ground black pepper
- ⅓ cup shredded Gruyère cheese
- ¼ cup crushed pork rinds

1. Salt the zucchini slices and put them in a colander in the sink for 45 minutes; the zucchini will shed much of their water.
2. Preheat the oven to 400°F.
3. When the zucchini have been "weeping" for about 30 minutes, in a small saucepan over medium-low heat, heat the Brie and butter, stirring occasionally, until the cheese has melted and the mixture is fully combined, about 2 minutes.
4. Arrange the zucchini in an 8-inch baking dish so the zucchini slices are overlapping a bit. Season with pepper.
5. Pour the Brie mixture over the zucchini, and top with the shredded Gruyère cheese.
6. Sprinkle the crushed pork rinds over the top.
7. Bake for about 25 minutes, until the dish is bubbling and the top is nicely browned, and serve.

PER SERVING

Calories: 355 | Total Fat: 25g | Carbs: 5g | Net Carbs: 4g | Fiber: 2g | Protein: 28g

Mug Biscuit

Prep time: 1 minutes | Cook time: 2 minutes |Serves 1

- ¼ cup (28 g) blanched almond flour
- 1 tablespoon coconut flour
- ½ teaspoon baking powder
- ¼ teaspoon finely ground sea salt
- 1 large egg
- 1 tablespoon softened coconut oil or ghee, plus more for serving if desired
- 1 teaspoon apple cider vinegar

1. Place all the ingredients in a microwave-safe mug with a base at least 2 inches (5 cm) in diameter. Mix until fully incorporated, then flatten with the back of a spoon.
2. Place the mug in the microwave and cook on high for 1 minute 30 seconds.
3. Remove the mug from the microwave and insert a toothpick. It should come out clean. If batter is clinging to the toothpick, microwave the biscuit for an additional 15 to 30 seconds.
4. Flip the mug over a clean plate and shake it a bit until the biscuit releases from the mug. If desired, slather the biscuit with the fat of your choice while still warm.

PER SERVING

Calories: 399 | Fat: 33.5 g |Carbs: 10.6 g | Dietary Fiber: 5.5 g | Net Carbs: 5.1 g | Sugars: 1.9 g | Protein: 13.8 g

Homemade Dairy Kefir

Prep time: 5 minutes, plus 18 to 24 hours to ferment | Cook time: 15 minutes | Makes 4 cups

- 4 cups organic whole milk
- 1 packet freeze-dried powdered kefir starter culture

1. Pour the milk into a clean quart-sized jar. Add the kefir starter and stir well.
2. Cover the jar with a coffee filter and seal with a rubber band around it. Leave it on the counter, away from direct sunlight, for 18 hours.
3. After 18 hours, uncover the kefir and smell it: if it's sour smelling and has thickened, it's ready to serve; if not, give it a few more hours. After 24 hours, remove the coffee filter and cover it with a lid. Store in the refrigerator for up to 2 weeks.

PER SERVING

Calories: 77 | Fat: 4g | Protein: 4g | Carbs: 4g | Fiber:0g | Net Carbs: 4g

Cheddar & Cream Cheese Chicken Casserole

Prep time: 30 minutes | Cook time: 23 minutes |Serves 4

- 2 tbsp olive oil
- 4 oz cream cheese, at room temperature
- 1 lb ground chicken
- ½ cup tomato sauce
- ½ cup natural yogurt
- 1 cup cheddar cheese, grated

1. Preheat oven to 350 F. Warm the oil in a skillet over medium heat and brown the chicken for a couple of minutes; set aside. Spread cream cheese at the bottom of a greased baking sheet, top with chicken, pour tomato sauce over, add yogurt dressing, and sprinkle with cheddar cheese.
2. Bake for 23 minutes until cheese has melted and golden brown on top.

PER SERVING

Calories: 512 | Fat: 38.6g | Net Carbs: 6.9g | Protein 32.3g

Lemon Coconut Cheesecake Fat Bombs

Prep time: 5 minutes | Cook time: 1 hour, 10 minutes | Serves 12

- 4 ounces full-fat cream cheese, softened
- ¼ cup coconut butter
- 3 tablespoons coconut flour
- 2 tablespoons monk fruit powdered sweetener
- Zest of 1 lemon
- Juice of ½ lemon
- ½ teaspoon vanilla extract

1. Line a baking sheet with parchment paper.
2. In a small bowl, beat the cream cheese and coconut butter together with a handheld or stand mixer.
3. Add the remaining and beat on medium speed until well combined.
4. Place the dough in the refrigerator to chill for 30 minutes.
5. Roll the dough into balls using 2 tablespoons of dough. Set the balls on the baking sheet. Repeat until all the dough is used.
6. Place the baking sheet in the freezer for 30 minutes, or until hard. Store in an airtight container in the freezer or in the refrigerator.

PER SERVING

Calories: 131 | Fat: 11.5g | Saturated Fat: 3.5g | Protein: 5.1g | Carbohydrate: 6.8g | Fiber: 1.5g | Sodium: 52mg

Favorite Onions Rings

Prep time: 5 minutes | Cook time: 20 minutes | Serves 4

- 1/2 cup coconut flour
- 3 eggs
- 2 tablespoons water
- 2 tablespoons double cream
- 4 ounces pork rinds
- 3 ounces parmesan cheese, grated
- 2 onions, cut into 1/2-inch thick rings

1. Place the coconut flour in a shallow dish. In another dish, mix the eggs, water, and cream; place the pork rinds and parmesan in the third dish.
2. Dip the onion rings into the coconut flour; then, dip them into the egg mixture; lastly, roll the onion rings in the parmesan mixture.
3. Place the coated rings on a lightly greased baking rack; bake at 420 degrees F for 13 to 16 minutes. Enjoy!

PER SERVING

Calories: 322 | Fat: 27.8g | Carbs: 5.7g | Protein: 10.1g | Fiber: 1g

Chocolate Pistachio Truffles

Prep time: 5 minutes | Cook time: 10 minutes | Serves 10

- 2/3 cup double cream
- 9 ounces sugar-free chocolate, chopped
- 1/4 teaspoon pure vanilla extract
- 1/4 cup pistachios, chopped
- 1/4 cup cocoa powder, unsweetened

1. Microwave the double cream for about 40 seconds. Add in the chocolate, vanilla, and pistachios
2. Mix until everything is well incorporated. Place the batter in the refrigerator for 1 hour.
3. Use a cookie scoop to roll your truffles into small balls.
4. Roll your truffles in the cocoa powder and serve. Bon appétit!

PER SERVING

Calories: 216 | Fat: 18g | Carbs: 6.7g | Protein: 5.1g | Fiber: 4.5g

Cultured Red Onion Relish

Prep time: 10 minutes, plus 4 days to ferment | Cook time: 15 minutes | Makes 3 cups drained

- ¼ teaspoon powdered starter culture for vegetables
- 2½ cups filtered water, divided
- 1 cup diced red radishes
- 1 cup diced red onions
- 1 cup seeded and diced cucumbers
- 1 tablespoon peeled and minced fresh ginger
- 1 tablespoon granulated erythritol
- 1 teaspoon kosher salt
- 2 sprigs fresh cilantro
- 3 whole cloves
- 2 whole allspice berries

1. Mix together the starter culture and ½ cup of the water in a medium-sized bowl and set aside.
2. Place the radishes, onions, cucumbers, ginger, sweetener, and salt in a large bowl and mix well. Stir in the cilantro, cloves, and allspice berries. Pack the vegetable mixture into a 1-quart jar, leaving 3 inches of space between the vegetables and the rim of the jar.
3. Add the starter culture mixture to the jar, then fill the jar with the remaining 2 cups of water until the vegetables are just covered.
4. Seal the jar and leave it on the counter, out of direct sunlight, for 4 days. Each day, open the jar and push any floating vegetables below the surface of the liquid, then reseal.
5. After the fourth day, the relish is ready to serve. Store in the refrigerator for up to 6 months.

PER SERVING

Calories: 8 | Fat: 0g | Protein: 0g | Carbs: 1.5g | Fiber: 0.5g | Net Carbs: 1g

Classic Blueberry Cheesecake

Prep time: 5 minutes | Cook time: 1 hour 10 minutes | Serves 2

- 4 tablespoons butter, room temperature
- 1/4 teaspoon ground star anise
- 1/2 cup almond flour Filling:
- 1/4 cup coconut-milk yogurt
- 4 ounces ricotta cheese, at room temperature
- 1/3 cup xylitol
- 1/2 teaspoon vanilla paste
- 2 eggs, whisked
- A handful of fresh blueberries

1. In a mixing bowl, thoroughly combine all of the crust ingredients.
2. Then, scrape the mixture into a lightly greased baking pan; place in your freezer for 30 minutes.
3. Then, mix the coconut-milk yogurt, ricotta cheese, xylitol, and vanilla using an electric mixer. Now, fold in the eggs, one at a time, mixing continuously until well blended. Pour the filling over the prepared crust.
4. degrees F and bake an additional 30 minutes.
5. Serve well chilled, garnished with fresh blueberries. Enjoy!

PER SERVING

Calories: 598 | Fat: 58.9g | Carbs: 7.4g | Protein: 13.3g | Fiber: 2g

Chia Protein Smoothie Bowl

Prep time: 5 minutes | **Cook time:** 5 minutes | Serves 2

- 2 tablespoons chia seeds
- 4 tablespoons peanut butter
- 1/2 cup coconut milk
- 4 tablespoons powdered erythritol
- A pinch of freshly grated nutmeg

1. Process all ingredients in your blender until well combined.
2. Pour into serving bowls and serve well-chilled. Enjoy!

PER SERVING

Calories: 280 | Fat: 16g | Carbs: 7g | Protein: 25g | Fiber: 4g

Caribbean-Style Chicken Wings

Prep time: 5 minutes | **Cook time:** 50 minutes | Serves 2

- 4 chicken wings
- 1 tablespoon coconut aminos
- 2 tablespoons rum
- 2 tablespoons butter
- 1 tablespoon onion powder
- 1 tablespoon garlic powder
- 1/2 teaspoon salt
- 1/4 teaspoon freshly ground black pepper
- 1/2 teaspoon red pepper flakes
- 1/4 teaspoon dried dill
- 1 tablespoons sesame seeds

1. Pat dry the chicken wings. Toss the chicken wings with the remaining ingredients until well coated. Arrange the chicken wings on a parchment-lined baking sheet.
2. Bake in the preheated oven at 420 degrees F for 45 minutes until golden brown.
3. Serve with your favorite sauce for dipping. Bon appétit!

PER SERVING

Calories: 286 | Fat: 18.5g | Carbs: 5.2g | Protein: 15.6g | Fiber: 1.9g

Walnut and Seed Crunch Bars

Prep time: 5 minutes | **Cook time:** 30 minutes | Serves 10

- 1/2 cup coconut flour
- 1/2 cup walnuts, ground
- 1/2 cup granulated Swerve
- 2/3 cup peanut butter, chunk-style
- 1/2 stick butter, softened
- 1 egg
- 1/4 cup hemp hearts
- 1/4 cup chia seeds

1. Mix the coconut flour with the walnuts and Swerve.
2. Add the wet mixture to the dry ingredients; stir in the hemp hearts and chia seeds.
3. Pour into a parchment-lined baking pan. Bake in the preheated oven at 360 degrees F for 11 to 13 minutes. Cut into bars and serve. Bon appétit!

PER SERVING

Calories: 190 | Fat: 17.1g | Carbs: 5.9g | Protein: 5.9g | Fiber: 2.7g

Roasted Radishes with Brown Butter Sauce

Prep time: 10 minutes | Cook time: 15 minutes | Serves 2

- 2 cups halved radishes
- 1 tablespoon olive oil
- Pink Himalayan salt
- Freshly ground black pepper
- 2 tablespoons butter
- 1 tablespoon chopped fresh flat-leaf Italian parsley

1. Preheat the oven to 450°F.
2. In a medium bowl, toss the radishes in the olive oil and season with pink Himalayan salt and pepper.
3. Spread the radishes on a baking sheet in a single layer. Roast for 15 minutes, stirring halfway through.
4. Meanwhile, when the radishes have been roasting for about 10 minutes, in a small, light-colored saucepan over medium heat, melt the butter completely, stirring frequently, and season with pink Himalayan salt. When the butter begins to bubble and foam, continue stirring. Transfer the browned butter to a heat-safe container (I use a mug).
5. Remove the radishes from the oven, and divide them between two plates. Spoon the brown butter over the radishes, top with the chopped parsley, and serve.

PER SERVING

Calories: 181 | Total Fat: 19g | Carbs: 4g | Net Carbs: 2g | Fiber: 2g | Protein: 1g

Herbed Kefir Cheese

Prep time: 5 minutes, plus 12 hours to drain | Cook time: 15 minutes | Makes 1 cup

- 2 cups full-fat unsweetened kefir, store-bought or homemade
- 1 ounce cream cheese (2 tablespoons), softened
- 1 tablespoon chopped fresh parsley
- 1 teaspoon minced garlic
- ½ teaspoon fresh thyme leaves
- ½ teaspoon kosher salt

1. Line a fine-mesh strainer with a large coffee filter. Set the strainer over a bowl and pour the kefir into the filter-lined strainer. Place in the fridge, uncovered, for 12 hours—longer if you want a firmer cheese.
2. When ready to use, discard the whey liquid and place the kefir cheese in a medium-sized bowl. Add the cream cheese and blend with a whisk or fork until smooth. Stir in the parsley, garlic, thyme, and salt until well blended. Chill for at least 1 hour before serving. Store the cheese in the refrigerator for up to 3 weeks.

PER SERVING

Calories: 52 | Fat: 3g | Protein: 4g | Carbs: 2g | Fiber: 0g | Net Carbs: 2g

Cheesy Chips with Avocado Dip

Prep time: 10 minutes | Cook time: 5 minutes |Serves 4

- 1 cup Parmesan cheese, grated
- ¼ tsp sweet paprika
- ¼ tsp Italian seasoning
- 2 soft avocados, pitted and scooped
- 1 tomato, chopped
- 1 tsp cilantro, chopped
- 1 tsp tabasco sauce
- Salt to taste

1. Preheat oven to 350 F and line a baking sheet with parchment paper.
2. Mix Parmesan cheese, Italian seasoning, and paprika. Make mounds on the baking sheet creating spaces between each mound. Flatten mounds. Bake for 5 minutes, let cool and remove to a plate.
3. To make the guacamole, mash avocado, with a fork in a bowl, add in tomato, cilantro, and tabasco sauce and continue to mash until mostly smooth; season with salt. Serve crackers with avocado dip.

PER SERVING

Calories: 283 | Fat: 22.4g | Net Carbs: 3.1g | Protein 12.7g

Cauliflower and Broccoli Cakes with Cheese

Prep time: 20 minutes | Cook time: 3 minutes |Serves 4

- ½ head broccoli, cut into florets
- ½ head cauliflower, cut into florets
- ½ cup Parmesan cheese, shredded
- ½ onion, chopped
- ½ cup almond flour
- 1 egg
- ½ tsp lemon juice
- 2 tbsp olive oil
- Salt and black pepper to taste
- 2 tbsp chives, chopped
- 2 tbsp Greek yogurt

1. Steam the cauliflower and broccoli in a pot filled with salted water for 10-12 minutes until tender. Drain and transfer to a bowl. Mash and add in the other ingredients, except for the olive oil. Season to taste and mix to combine.
2. Place a skillet over medium heat and heat olive oil. Shape fritters out of the mixture. Fry for 3 minutes per side. Garnish with Greek yogurt; sprinkle with chives.

PER SERVING

Calories: 155 | Fat: 15.5g | Net Carbs: 4.2g | Protein 5.5g

Cheese and Bacon Fat Bombs

Prep time: 5 minutes | Cook time: 1 hour 5 minutes |Serves 10

- 1/2 stick butter, at room temperature
- 8 ounces cottage cheese, at room temperature
- 8 ounces mozzarella cheese, crumbled
- 1 teaspoon shallot powder
- 1 teaspoon Italian seasoning blend
- 2 ounces bacon bits

1. Mix the butter, cheese, shallot powder, and Italian seasoning blend until well combined.
2. Place the mixture in your refrigerator for about 60 minutes.
3. Shape the mixture into 18 balls. Roll each ball in the bacon bits until coated on all sides. Enjoy!

PER SERVING

Calories: 149 | Fat: 9.3g | Carbs: 2.2g | Protein: 13.1g | Fiber: 0.6g

Spicy Roasted Pumpkin Seeds

Prep time: 5 minutes | Cook time: 10 minutes | Serves 8

- 4 tablespoons coconut oil
- 2 cups raw pumpkin seeds
- 4 teaspoons Tabasco sauce
- ½ teaspoon cayenne pepper

1. Line a baking sheet with parchment paper.
2. Heat the oil in a large pan over medium heat.
3. Add the pumpkin seeds and sauté for 2 to 3 minutes, or until they start to pop and turn golden brown.
4. Add the Tabasco and cayenne, toss, and continue to cook for 1 minute.
5. Transfer to the baking sheet, carefully spread the seeds out in a single layer, and let cool before serving. Store in a glass container at room temperature.

PER SERVING

Calories: 246 | Fat: 22.7g | Saturated Fat: 8.9g | Protein: 8.5g | Carbohydrate: 6.2g | Fiber: 1.4g | Sodium: 21mg

Vanilla Custard Pudding

Prep time: 5 minutes | Cook time: 25 minutes | Serves 4

- 2 eggs
- A pinch of flaky salt
- 2 egg yolks
- 1 vanilla bean
- 4 tablespoons granulated Swerve
- 1 ½ cups heavy whipping cream
- 1/4 teaspoon ground cloves
- 1/4 teaspoon ground cinnamon

1. Carefully separate the egg whites from the yolks. Whip the egg whites just until a bit foamy. Add in a pinch of salt and beat the eggs until soft peaks have formed. Set aside.
2. In a sauté pan, place the egg yolks, vanilla, Swerve and cream. Let it simmer over moderate flame until thickened and thoroughly heated, about 20 minutes. Add in the ground cloves and cinnamon; mix again to combine well.
3. Remove from the heat and fold in the reserved egg whites; gently stir to combine and let it cool to room temperature.
4. Place in your refrigerator until ready to use. Devour!

PER SERVING

Calories: 214 | Fat: 21g | Carbs: 1.7g | Protein: 5g | Fiber: 0g

Fried Artichokes with Pesto

Prep time: 20 minutes | Cook time: 5 minutes | Serves 4

- 2 tbsp olive oil
- 12 fresh baby artichokes
- 2 tbsp lemon juice
- 1 tbsp vinegar
- 4 tbsp pesto
- Salt to taste

1. Place the artichokes in cold water with vinegar for 10 minutes. Drain and pat dry well with kitchen towels. Cut the artichokes down the middle vertically, and with a teaspoon, scoop out the stringy stifle to uncover the heart. Slice the artichokes vertically into narrow wedges.
2. Heat olive oil in a skillet over high heat. Fry the artichokes until browned and crispy. Drain excess oil using paper towels. Sprinkle with salt and lemon juice and serve with pesto.

PER SERVING

Calories: 235 | Fat: 17.4g | Net Carbs: 8.7g | Protein 8.2g

Parmesan and Pork Rind Green Beans

Prep time: 5 minutes | Cook time: 15 minutes | Serves 2

- ½ pound fresh green beans
- 2 tablespoons crushed pork rinds
- 2 tablespoons olive oil
- 1 tablespoon grated Parmesan cheese
- Pink Himalayan salt
- Freshly ground black pepper

1. Preheat the oven to 400°F.
2. In a medium bowl, combine the green beans, pork rinds, olive oil, and Parmesan cheese. Season with pink Himalayan salt and pepper, and toss until the beans are thoroughly coated.
3. Spread the bean mixture on a baking sheet in a single layer, and roast for about 15 minutes. At the halfway point, give the pan a little shake to move the beans around, or just give them a stir.
4. Divide the beans between two plates and serve.

PER SERVING

Calories: 175 | Total Fat: 15g | Carbs: 8g | Net Carbs: 5g | Fiber: 3g | Protein: 6g

Golden Flax Seed and Pecan Pudding

Prep time: 5 minutes | Cook time: 10 minutes | Serves 2

- 2/3 cup water
- 1/2 cup canned coconut milk
- 2 tablespoons pecans, ground
- 2 tablespoons coconut flour
- 2 tablespoons golden flaxseeds, ground
- A few drops of liquid Stevia
- A pinch of grated nutmeg

1. Place the water and coconut milk in a sauté pan over medium-high heat; bring to a boil.
2. Add in the remaining items. Turn the heat to medium-low and cook, stirring frequently, for 2 minutes or until thoroughly heated.
3. Divide between two serving bowls and let it cool at room temperature.
4. Transfer to your refrigerator and serve well-chilled. Enjoy!

PER SERVING

Calories: 327 | Fat: 32g | Carbs: 6.7g | Protein: 4.8g | Fiber: 4.9g

Spanish Piquillo Peppers with Cheese Stuffing

Prep time: 20 minutes | Cook time: 10 minutes |Serves 4

- 4 canned roasted piquillo peppers
- 2 tbsp olive oil
- 1 tbsp parsley, chopped
- Filling
- 4 ounces goat cheese
- 2 tbsp heavy cream
- 1 tbsp olive oil

1. Preheat the oven to 350 F and grease a baking sheet with some olive oil. Mix all filling ingredients in a bowl. Place in a freezer bag, press down and squeeze, and cut off the bottom.
2. Drain and deseed the peppers. Squeeze about 2 tbsp of the filling into each pepper. Arrange them on the baking sheet, drizzle over the remaining olive oil and bake for 10 minutes.

PER SERVING

Calories: 274 | Fat: 24.3g | Net Carbs: 4.2g | Protein 11g

Buttery Slow-Cooker Mushrooms

Prep time: 10 minutes | Cook time: 4 hours | Serves 2

- 6 tablespoons butter
- 1 tablespoon packaged dry ranch-dressing mix
- 8 ounces fresh cremini mushrooms
- 2 tablespoons grated Parmesan cheese
- 1 tablespoon chopped fresh flat-leaf Italian parsley

1. with the crock insert in place, preheat the slow cooker to low.
2. Put the butter and the dry ranch dressing in the bottom of the slow cooker, and allow the butter to melt. Stir to blend the dressing mix and butter.
3. Add the mushrooms to the slow cooker, and stir to coat with the butter-dressing mixture. Sprinkle the top with the Parmesan cheese.
4. Cover and cook on low for 4 hours.
5. Use a slotted spoon to transfer the mushrooms to a serving dish. Top with the chopped parsley and serve.

PER SERVING

Calories: 351 | Total Fat: 36g | Carbs: 5g | Net Carbs: 4g | Fiber: 1g | Protein: 6g

No-Bake Cheesecake Truffles

Prep time: 5 minutes | Cook time:10 minutes |Serves 10

- 2 ounces butter, at room temperature
- 9 ounces mascarpone cheese, at room temperature
- 2 cups powdered erythritol
- 9 ounces sugar-free chocolate chips
- 1 tablespoon powdered erythritol
- 1 tablespoon cocoa powder, unsweetened
- 1/2 teaspoon chipotle powder

1. Thoroughly combine the softened butter with cheese, 2 cups of powdered erythritol, chocolate, and butterscotch extract. Place the mixture in the refrigerator for 2 hours.
2. Roll the batter into balls.
3. Mix all ingredients for the coating. Roll the balls into coating powder and place in your refrigerator until ready to use. Bon appétit!

PER SERVING

Calories: 293 | Fat: 26g | Carbs: 5.6g | Protein: 5.3g | Fiber: 1g

Chapter 5

Poultry

Buttery Garlic Chicken

Prep time: 5 minutes | Cook time: 40 minutes | Serves 2

- 2 tablespoons ghee, melted
- 2 boneless skinless chicken breasts
- Pink Himalayan salt
- Freshly ground black pepper
- 1 tablespoon dried Italian seasoning
- 4 tablespoons butter
- 2 garlic cloves, minced
- ¼ cup grated Parmesan cheese

1. Preheat the oven to 375°F. Choose a baking dish that is large enough to hold both chicken breasts and coat it with the ghee.
2. Pat dry the chicken breasts and season with pink Himalayan salt, pepper, and Italian seasoning. Place the chicken in the baking dish.
3. In a medium skillet over medium heat, melt the butter. Add the minced garlic, and cook for about 5 minutes. You want the garlic very lightly browned but not burned.
4. Remove the butter-garlic mixture from the heat, and pour it over the chicken breasts.
5. Roast the chicken in the oven for 30 to 35 minutes, until cooked through. Sprinkle some of the Parmesan cheese on top of each chicken breast. Let the chicken rest in the baking dish for 5 minutes.
6. Divide the chicken between two plates, spoon the butter sauce over the chicken, and serve.

PER SERVING

Calories: 642 | Total Fat: 45g | Carbs: 2g | Net Carbs: 2g | Fiber: 0g | Protein: 57g

Parmesan Baked Chicken

Prep time: 5 minutes | Cook time: 20 minutes | Serves 2

- 2 tablespoons ghee
- 2 boneless skinless chicken breasts
- Pink Himalayan salt
- Freshly ground black pepper
- ½ cup mayonnaise
- ¼ cup grated Parmesan cheese
- 1 tablespoon dried Italian seasoning
- ¼ cup crushed pork rinds

1. Preheat the oven to 425°F. Choose a baking dish that is large enough to hold both chicken breasts and coat it with the ghee.
2. Pat dry the chicken breasts with a paper towel, season with pink Himalayan salt and pepper, and place in the prepared baking dish.
3. In a small bowl, mix to combine the mayonnaise, Parmesan cheese, and Italian seasoning.
4. Slather the mayonnaise mixture evenly over the chicken breasts, and sprinkle the crushed pork rinds on top of the mayonnaise mixture.
5. Bake until the topping is browned, about 20 minutes, and serve.

PER SERVING

Calories: 850 | Total Fat: 67g | Carbs: 2g | Net Carbs: 2g | Fiber: 0g | Protein: 60g

Sauced Chicken Legs with Vegetables

Prep time: 60 minutes | Cook time: 35 minutes | Serves 4

- 2 tbsp olive oil
- 1 parsnip, chopped
- 2 celery stalks, chopped
- 2 cups chicken stock
- 1 onion, chopped
- ¼ cup red wine
- 1 pound chicken legs
- 1 cup tomatoes, chopped
- 1 cup spinach
- ¼ tsp dried thyme
- Salt and black pepper, to taste
- 1 tbsp parsley, chopped

1. Put a pot over medium heat and heat the olive oil. Add garlic, parsnip, celery, and onion; season with salt and pepper and sauté for 5-6 minutes until tender. Stir in the chicken and cook for 5 minutes.
2. Pour in the stock, tomatoes, and thyme, and cook for 30 minutes. Sprinkle with parsley to serve.

PER SERVING

Calories: 264 | Fat: 14,5g | Net Carbs: 7.1g | Protein 22.5g

Baked Zucchini with Chicken and Cheese

Prep time: 45 minutes | Cook time: 35 minutes | Serves 4

- 1 pound chicken breasts, cubed
- 1 tbsp butter
- 1 tbsp olive oil
- 1 red bell pepper, chopped
- 1 shallot, sliced
- 2 zucchinis, cubed
- 1 garlic clove, minced
- 1 tsp thyme
- Salt and black pepper to taste
- ½ cup cream cheese, softened
- ¼ cup mayonnaise
- 1 tbsp Worcestershire sauce (sugar-free)
- 1 cup mozzarella cheese, shredded

1. Set oven to 370 F and grease and line a baking dish. Heat the butter and olive oil in a pan over medium heat and add in the chicken.
2. Cook until lightly browned, for about 5 minutes. Place in shallot, zucchini cubes, black pepper, garlic, bell pepper, salt, and thyme. Cook until tender and set aside.
3. In a bowl, mix cream cheese, mayonnaise, and Worcestershire sauce. Stir in meat and sauteed vegetables. Place the mixture into the prepared baking dish and bake for 20 minutes. Then, sprinkle with the mozzarella cheese and bake until browned for 10 more minutes.

PER SERVING

Calories: 488 | Fat: 38.3g | Net Carbs: 5.2g | Protein 23.3g

Teriyaki Chicken Wings with Spring Onions

Prep time: 40 minutes | Cook time: 35 minutes |Serves 4

- 2 tbsp sesame oil
- 1 pound chicken wings
- 4 tbsp teriyaki sauce
- Salt to taste
- Chili sauce to taste
- Lemon juice from 1 lemon
- 2 spring onions, sliced

1. Preheat oven to 390 F. In a bowl, mix the teriyaki sauce, olive oil, salt, chili sauce, and lemon juice.
2. Add in the wings and toss to coat. Place the chicken in a roasting dish lined with parchment paper and roast for 35 minutes, turning once halfway. Garnish with spring onions to serve.

PER SERVING

Calories: 177 | Fat: 11g | Net Carbs: 4.3g | Protein 21g

Turkey Stew with Salsa Verde

Prep time: 30 minutes | Cook time: 20 minutes | Serves 6

- 4 cups leftover turkey meat, chopped
- 2 cups green beans
- 6 cups chicken stock
- Salt and ground black pepper, to taste
- 1 fresh chipotle pepper, chopped
- ½ cup salsa verde
- 1 tsp ground coriander
- 2 tsp cumin
- ¼ cup sour cream
- 1 tbsp fresh cilantro, chopped

1. Set a pan over medium heat. Add in the stock and heat. Stir in green beans, and cook for 10 minutes. Place in the turkey, ground coriander, salt, salsa verde, chipotle pepper, cumin, and black pepper, and cook for 10 minutes.
2. Stir in the sour cream, kill the heat, and separate into bowls. Top with chopped cilantro to serve.

PER SERVING

Calories: 193 | Fat: 11g | Net Carbs: 2g | Protein: 27

Lemon Threaded Chicken Skewers

Prep time: 2 hours 17 minutes | Cook time: 5 minutes | Serves 4

- 3 chicken breasts, cut into cubes
- 2 tbsp olive oil, divided
- 2/3 jar preserved lemon, flesh removed, drained
- ½ cup lemon juice
- Salt and black pepper to taste
- 1 tsp rosemary leaves to garnish
- 2 to 4 lemon wedges to garnish

1. First, thread the chicken onto skewers and set aside.
2. In a wide bowl, mix half of the oil, garlic, salt, pepper, and lemon juice, and add the chicken skewers, and lemon rind. Cover the bowl and let the chicken marinate for at least 2 hours in the refrigerator.
3. When the marinating time is almost over, preheat a grill to 350°F, and remove the chicken onto the grill. Cook for 6 minutes on each side.
4. Remove and serve warm garnished with rosemary leaves and lemons wedges.

PER SERVING

Calories: 350 | Fat: 11g | Net Carbs: 3.5g | Protein: 34g

Delicious Chicken Puttanesca

Prep time: 5 minutes | Cook time: 25 minutes |Serves 5

- 2 tablespoons olive oil
- 1 bell pepper, chopped
- 1 red onion, chopped
- 1 teaspoon garlic, minced
- 1½ pounds chicken wings, boneless
- 2 cups tomato sauce
- 1 tablespoon capers
- 1/4 teaspoon red pepper, crushed
- 1/4 cup parmesan cheese, preferably freshly grated
- 2 basil sprigs, chopped

1. Heat the olive oil in a non-stick skillet over a moderate flame. Once hot, sauté the bell peppers and onions until tender and fragrant.
2. Stir in the garlic and continue to cook an additional 30 seconds.
3. Stir in the chicken wings, tomato sauce, capers, and red pepper; continue to cook for a further 20 minutes or until everything is heated through.
4. Serve garnished with freshly grated parmesan and basil. Bon appétit!

PER SERVING

Calories: 265 | Fat:11.4g | Carbs: 6.5g | Protein: 32.5g | Fiber: 1.4g

Creamy Stuffed Chicken with Parma Ham

Prep time: 40 minutes | Cook time: 5 minutes | Serves 4

- 4 chicken breasts
- tbsp olive oil
- cloves garlic, minced
- shallots, finely chopped
- tbsp dried mixed herbs
- 8 slices Parma ham
- 8 oz cream cheese
- 2 lemons, zested Salt to taste

1. Preheat the oven to 350°F.
2. Heat the oil in a small skillet and sauté the garlic and shallots with a pinch of salt and lemon zest for 3 minutes; let it cool. After, stir the cream cheese and mixed herbs into the shallot mixture.
3. Score a pocket in each chicken breast, fill the holes with the cream cheese mixture and cover with the cut-out chicken. Wrap each breast with two Parma ham and secure the ends with a toothpick. Lay the chicken parcels on a greased baking sheet and cook in the oven for 20 minutes. Remove to rest for 4 minutes before serving with green salad and roasted tomatoes.

PER SERVING

Calories: 485 | Fat: 35g | Net Carbs: 2g | Protein: 26g

Fried Chicken with Coconut Sauce

Prep time: 30 minutes | Cook time: 15 minutes | Serves 6

- 1 tbsp coconut oil
- 3 ½ pounds chicken breasts
- 1 cup chicken stock
- 1¼ cups leeks, chopped
- 1 tbsp lime juice
- ¼ cup coconut cream
- 2 tsp paprika
- tsp red pepper flakes
- tbsp green onions, chopped for garnishing
- Salt and ground black pepper, to taste

1. Set a pan over medium heat and warm oil, place in the chicken, cook each side for 2 minutes, set to a plate, and set aside. Set heat to medium, place the leeks to the pan and cook for 4 minutes.
2. Stir in the black pepper, stock, pepper flakes, salt, paprika, coconut cream, and lime juice. Take the chicken back to the pan, season with some more pepper and salt, and cook covered for 15 minutes.

PER SERVING

Calories: 491 | Fat: 35g | Net Carbs: 3.2g | Protein: 58g

Creamy Slow-Cooker Chicken

Prep time: 10 minutes | Cook time: 4 hours 15 minutes | Serves 2

- 1 tablespoon ghee
- 2 boneless skinless chicken breasts
- 1 cup Alfredo Sauce, or any brand you like
- ¼ cup chopped sun-dried tomatoes
- ¼ cup grated Parmesan cheese
- Pink Himalayan salt
- Freshly ground black pepper
- 2 cups fresh spinach

1. In a medium skillet over medium-high heat, melt the ghee. Add the chicken and cook, about 4 minutes on each side, until brown.
2. with the crock insert in place, transfer the chicken to the slow cooker. Set the slow cooker to low.
3. Cover and cook on low for 4 hours, or until the chicken is cooked through.
4. Add the fresh spinach. Cover and cook for 5 minutes more, until the spinach is slightly wilted, and serve.

PER SERVING

Calories: 900 | Total Fat: 66g | Carbs: 9g | Net Carbs: 7g | Fiber: 2g | Protein: 70g

Cheesy Turkey Sausage Egg Muffins

Prep time: 15 minutes | Cook time: 5 minutes | Serves 3

- 1 tsp butter
- ½ tsp dried rosemary
- 1 cup pecorino romano cheese, grated
- 3 turkey sausages, chopped

1. Preheat oven to 400°F and grease muffin cups with cooking spray.
2. In a skillet over medium heat add the butter and cook the turkey sausages for 4-5 minutes.
3. Beat 3 eggs with a fork. Add in sausages, cheese, and seasonings. Divide between the muffin cups and bake for 4 minutes. Crack in an egg to each of the cups. Bake for an additional 4 minutes. Allow cooling before serving.

PER SERVING

Calories: 423 | Fat: 34.1g | Net Carbs: 2.2g | Protein: 26.5g

Italian-Seasoned Turkey Breasts

Prep time: 5 minutes | Cook time: 20 minutes | Serves 5

- 2 eggs
- 1 cup sour cream
- 1 teaspoon Italian seasoning blend
- Kosher salt and ground black pepper, to taste
- 1/2 cup grated parmesan cheese
- 2 pounds turkey fillets

1. In a mixing bowl, whisk the eggs until frothy and light. Stir in the sour cream and continue whisking until well combined.
2. In another bowl, mix the Italian seasoning blend with the salt, black pepper, and parmesan cheese; mix to combine well.
3. Dip the turkey fillets into the egg mixture; then, press them into the parmesan mixture.
4. Cook in the greased frying pan until browned on all sides. Bon appétit!

PER SERVING

Calories: 335 | Fat: 12.8g | Carbs: 5.3g | Protein: 47.7g | Fiber: 0.1g

Chicken with Parmesan Topping

Prep time: 45 minutes | Cook time: 5 minutes | Serves 4

- chicken breast halves, skinless and boneless
- Salt and black pepper, to taste
- ¼ cup green chilies, chopped
- bacon slices, chopped
- ounces cream cheese
- ¼ cup onion, chopped
- ½ cup mayonnaise
- ½ cup Grana Padano cheese, grated
- 1 cup cheddar cheese, grated
- 2 ounces pork rinds, crushed
- 2 tbsp olive oil
- ½ cup Parmesan cheese, shredded

1. Season the chicken with salt and pepper. Heat the olive oil in a pan over medium heat and fry the chicken for approximately 4-6 minutes until cooked through with no pink showing. Remove to a baking dish.
2. In the same pan, fry bacon until crispy and remove to a plate. Sauté the onion for 3 minutes, until soft. Remove from heat, add in the fried bacon, cream cheese, 1 cup of water, Grana Padano cheese, mayonnaise, chilies, and cheddar cheese, and spread over the chicken.
3. Bake in the oven for 10-15 minutes at 370°F. Remove and sprinkle with mixed Parmesan cheese and pork rinds and return to the oven. Bake for another 10-15 minutes until the cheese melts. Serve immediately.

PER SERVING

Calories: 361 | Fat: 15g | Net Carbs: 5g | Protein: 25g

Traditional Hungarian Paprikash

Prep time: 5 minutes | Cook time: 35 minutes |Serves 5

- 2 tablespoons olive oil
- 2 pounds chicken drumsticks
- 1/2 cup leeks, sliced
- 1 bell pepper, deseeded and chopped
- 1 Hungarian wax pepper, chopped
- 3 garlic cloves, chopped
- 1 cup tomato puree
- 4 cups vegetable broth
- 1 tablespoon Hungarian paprika
- 1 bay laurel

1. Heat the olive oil in a soup pot over a moderate flame. Once hot, brown the chicken drumsticks for about 7 minutes or until no longer pink; shred the meat and reserve.
2. Then, cook the leeks and peppers in the pan drippings for about 5 minutes or until they have softened.
3. Now, add in the garlic and cook for a minute or so. Add in the tomato puree, vegetable broth, salt, black pepper, Hungarian paprika, and bay laurel.
4. Stir in the reserved chicken and bring to a boil; turn the heat to medium-low, cover, and let it simmer for 22 minutes.
5. Ladle into individual bowls and serve. Enjoy!

PER SERVING

Calories: 358 | Fat: 22.2g | Carbs: 4.4g | Protein: 33.3g | Fiber: 0.7g

Baked Garlic and Paprika Chicken Legs

Prep time: 10 minutes | Cook time: 55 minutes | Serves 2

- 1 pound chicken drumsticks, skin on
- Pink Himalayan salt
- Freshly ground black pepper
- 2 tablespoons ghee
- 2 garlic cloves, minced
- 1 teaspoon paprika
- 1 teaspoon dried Italian seasoning
- ½ pound fresh green beans
- 1 tablespoon olive oil

1. Preheat the oven to 425°F. Line a 9-by-13-inch baking pan with aluminum foil or a silicone baking mat.
2. Pat the chicken legs dry with paper towels, put them in a large bowl, and apply pink Himalayan salt and pepper all over the skin on both sides.
3. In a small saucepan over medium-low heat, combine the ghee, garlic, paprika, and Italian seasoning. Stir to combine for 30 seconds, and let sit for 5 minutes while the flavors combine.
4. Pour the sauce over the chicken legs, and toss to coat evenly. Season with more pink Himalayan salt and pepper.
5. Arrange the chicken legs on one side of the prepared pan, leaving room for the vegetables later.
6. Bake the chicken for 30 minutes, then remove the pan from the oven. Spread the green beans over the empty half of the pan, and turn the chicken legs. Drizzle the beans with the olive oil, and season with pink Himalayan salt and pepper.
7. Roast for 15 to 20 minutes more, until the chicken is cooked through and the skin is crispy, and serve.

PER SERVING

Calories: 700 | Total Fat: 45g | Carbs: 10g | Net Carbs: 6g | Fiber: 4g | Protein: 63g

Tangy Classic Chicken Drumettes

Prep time: 5 minutes | Cook time: 40 minutes |Serves 4

- 1 pound chicken drumettes
- 1 tablespoon olive oil
- 2 tablespoons butter, melted
- 1 garlic cloves, sliced
- Fresh juice of 1/2 lemon
- 2 tablespoons white wine
- Salt and ground black pepper, to taste
- 1 tablespoon fresh scallions, chopped

1. Start by preheating your oven to 440 degrees F. Place the chicken in a parchment-lined baking pan. Drizzle with olive oil and melted butter.
2. Add the garlic, lemon, wine, salt, and black pepper.
3. Bake in the preheated oven for about 35 minutes. Serve garnished with fresh scallions. Enjoy!

PER SERVING

Calories: 209 | Fat: 12.2g | Carbs: 0.4g | Fiber: 0.1g | Protein: 23.2g

Paprika Chicken Sandwiches

Prep time: 5 minutes | Cook time:20 minutes |Serves 1

Buns:
- 2 pounds (910 g) boneless, skinless chicken thighs
- ¼ cup (55 g) coconut oil, or ¼ cup (60 ml) avocado oil

Sauce:
- ⅓ cup (70 g) mayonnaise
- 2 teaspoons lemon juice
- 1 clove garlic, minced
- ¾ teaspoon paprika
- ¼ teaspoon ground black pepper

Sandwich Fillings:
- ½ cup (35 g) fresh spinach
- 8 fresh basil leaves
- 4 ounces (115 g) salami, sliced

1. Place the chicken thighs on a sheet of parchment paper. (Note: If your package of chicken thighs did not give you 8 thighs, cut the largest thigh[s] in half until you have 8 pieces.) Using a meat mallet, pound the thighs until they're ¼ inch (6 mm) thick.
2. Heat the oil in a large frying pan over medium-low heat. Add the chicken and cook for 10 minutes, then turn the chicken over and cook for another 10 minutes, or until both sides are golden and the internal temperature reaches 165°F (74°C).
3. When the chicken is done, divide evenly among 4 plates, 2 pieces per plate.
4. To assemble, spread one-quarter of the sauce on one piece of chicken on each plate, then top each sauced chicken piece with one-quarter of the spinach, 2 basil leaves, and 1 ounce (28 g) of salami. Top with the second chicken piece to make sandwiches.

PER SERVING

Calories: 870 | Fat: 72.1 g | Carbs: 3 g | Dietary Fiber: 0.8 g | Net Carbs: 2.2 g | Sugars: 1.1 g | Protein: 52.3 g

Cheddar Chicken Tenders

Prep time: 40 minutes | Cook time: 25 minutes | Serves 4

- eggs
- tbsp butter, melted
- 3 cups coarsely crushed cheddar cheese
- ½ cup pork rinds, crushed
- 1 lb chicken tenders
- Pink salt to taste

1. Preheat oven to 350°F and line a baking sheet with parchment paper. Whisk the eggs with the butter in one bowl and mix the cheese and pork rinds in another bowl.
2. Season chicken with salt, dip in egg mixture, and coat generously in cheddar mixture. Place on the baking sheet, cover with aluminium foil and bake for 25 minutes. Remove foil and bake further for 12 minutes to golden brown. Serve chicken with mustard dip.

PER SERVING

Calories: 507 | Fat: 54g | Net Carbs: 1.3g | Protein: 42g

Chicken Cauliflower Bake

Prep time: 58 minutes | Cook time: 5 minutes | Serves 6

- 3 cups cubed leftover chicken
- 3 cups spinach
- cauliflower heads, cut into florets
- cups water
- 3 eggs, lightly beaten
- 2 cups grated sharp cheddar cheese
- 1 cup pork rinds, crushed
- ½ cup unsweetened almond milk
- 3 tbsp olive oil
- 3 cloves garlic, minced
- Salt and black pepper to taste
- Cooking spray

1. Preheat the oven to 350°F and grease a baking dish with cooking spray. Set aside.
2. Pour the cauli florets and water in a pot; bring to boil over medium heat. Cover and steam the cauli florets for 8 minutes. Drain them through a colander and set aside.
3. Also, combine the cheddar cheese and pork rinds in a large bowl and mix in the chicken. Set aside.
4. Heat the olive oil in a skillet and cook the garlic and spinach until the spinach has wilted, about 5 minutes. Season with salt and black pepper, and add the spinach mixture and cauli florets to the chicken bowl.
5. Top with the eggs and almond milk, mix and transfer everything to the baking dish. Layer the top of the ingredients and place the dish in the oven to bake for 30 minutes.
6. By this time the edges and top must have browned nicely, then remove the chicken from the oven, let rest for 5 minutes, and serve. Garnish with steamed and seasoned green beans.

PER SERVING

Calories: 390 | Fat: 27g | Net Carbs: 3g | Protein: 22g

Crunchy Chicken Milanese

Prep time: 10 minutes | Cook time: 10 minutes | Serves 2

- 2 boneless skinless chicken breasts
- ½ cup coconut flour
- 1 teaspoon ground cayenne pepper
- Pink Himalayan salt
- Freshly ground black pepper
- 1 egg, lightly beaten
- ½ cup crushed pork rinds
- 2 tablespoons olive oil

1. Pound the chicken breasts with a heavy mallet until they are about ½ inch thick. (If you don't have a kitchen mallet, you can use the thick rim of a heavy plate.)
2. Prepare two separate prep plates and one small, shallow bowl:
3. •On plate 1, put the coconut flour, cayenne pepper, pink Himalayan salt, and pepper. Mix together.
4. •Crack the egg into the small bowl, and lightly beat it with a fork or whisk.
5. •On plate 2, put the crushed pork rinds.
6. In a large skillet over medium-high heat, heat the olive oil.
7. Dredge 1 chicken breast on both sides in the coconut-flour mixture. Dip the chicken into the egg, and coat both sides. Dredge the chicken in the pork-rind mixture, pressing the pork rinds into the chicken so they stick. Place the coated chicken in the hot skillet and repeat with the other chicken breast.
8. Cook the chicken for 3 to 5 minutes on each side, until brown, crispy, and cooked through, and serve.

PER SERVING

Calories: 604 | Total Fat: 29g | Carbs: 17g | Net Carbs: 7g | Fiber: 10g | Protein: 65g

Zesty Grilled Chicken

Prep time: 35 minutes | Cook time: 20 minutes | Serves 8

- 2½ pounds chicken thighs and drumsticks
- 1 tbsp coconut aminos
- 1 tbsp apple cider vinegar
- A pinch of red pepper flakes
- Salt and black pepper, to taste
- ½ tsp ground ginger
- ⅓ cup butter
- 1 garlic clove, minced
- 1 tsp lime zest
- ½ cup warm water

1. In a blender, combine the butter with water, salt, ginger, vinegar, garlic, pepper, lime zest, aminos, and pepper flakes. Pat the chicken dry, lay on a pan, and top with zesty marinade. Refrigerate for 1 hour.
2. Set the chicken pieces skin side down on a preheated grill over medium heat, cook for 10 minutes, turn, brush with some marinade, and cook for 10 minutes. Split among serving plates and enjoy.

PER SERVING

Calories: 375 | Fat: 12g | Net Carbs: 3g | Protein: 42g

Chicken with Monterey Jack Cheese

Prep time: 30 minutes | Cook time: 15 minutes | Serves 3

- 2 tbsp butter
- 1 tsp garlic, minced
- 1 pound chicken breasts
- 1 tsp creole seasoning
- ¼ cup scallions, chopped
- ½ cup tomatoes, chopped
- ½ cup chicken stock
- ¼ cup whipping cream
- ½ cup Monterey Jack cheese, grated
- ¼ cup fresh cilantro, chopped
- Salt and black pepper, to taste
- 4 ounces cream cheese
- 8 eggs
- A pinch of garlic powder

1. Set a pan over medium heat and warm 1 tbsp butter. Add chicken, season with creole seasoning and cook each side for 2 minutes; remove to a plate. Melt the rest of the butter and stir in garlic and tomatoes; cook for 4 minutes. Return the chicken to the pan and pour in stock; cook for 15 minutes. Place in whipping cream, scallions, salt, Monterey Jack cheese, and pepper; cook for 2 minutes.
2. In a blender, combine the cream cheese with garlic powder, salt, eggs, and pepper, and pulse well. Place the mixture into a lined baking sheet, and at 325°F. Allow the cheese sheet to cool down, place on a cutting board, roll, and slice into medium slices. Split the slices among bowls and top with chicken mixture. Sprinkle with chopped cilantro to serve.

PER SERVING

Calories: 445 | Fat: 34g | Net Carbs: 4g | Protein: 39g

Cheesy Bacon and Broccoli Chicken

Prep time: 10 minutes | Cook time: 1 hour | Serves 2

- 2 tablespoons ghee
- 2 boneless skinless chicken breasts
- Pink Himalayan salt
- Freshly ground black pepper
- 4 bacon slices
- 6 ounces cream cheese, at room temperature
- 2 cups frozen broccoli florets, thawed
- ½ cup shredded Cheddar cheese

1. Preheat the oven to 375°F.
2. Choose a baking dish that is large enough to hold both chicken breasts and coat it with the ghee.
3. Pat dry the chicken breasts with a paper towel, and season with pink Himalayan salt and pepper.
4. Place the chicken breasts and the bacon slices in the baking dish, and bake for 25 minutes.
5. Transfer the chicken to a cutting board and use two forks to shred it. Season it again with pink Himalayan salt and pepper.
6. Place the bacon on a paper towel-lined plate to crisp up, and then crumble it.
7. In a medium bowl, mix to combine the cream cheese, shredded chicken, broccoli, and half of the bacon crumbles. Transfer the chicken mixture to the baking dish, and top with the Cheddar and the remaining half of the bacon crumbles.
8. Bake until the cheese is bubbling and browned, about 35 minutes, and serve.

PER SERVING

Calories: 935 | Total Fat: 66g | Carbs: 10g | Net Carbs: 8g | Fiber: 3g | Protein: 75g

Grilled Chicken with Broccoli & Carrots

Prep time: 17 minutes | Cook time: 7 minutes | Serves 4

- 2 tbsp olive oil
- 1 tbsp smoked paprika
- Salt and black pepper to taste
- 1 tsp garlic powder
- 2 pounds chicken breasts
- 1 small head broccoli, cut into florets
- 2 baby carrots, sliced

1. Put broccoli florets and carrots into the steamer basket over the boiling water. Steam for about 8 minutes or until crisp-tender. Set aside to cool, then sprinkle with salt and olive oil.
2. Grease grill grate with cooking spray and preheat to 400 F.
3. Combine paprika, salt, pepper, and garlic powder in a bowl. Brush chicken with olive oil and sprinkle spice mixture over; massage with hands. Grill chicken for 7 minutes per side until well-cooked, and plate. Serve with steamed vegetables.

PER SERVING

Calories: 466 | Fat: 29g | Net Carbs: 1.9g | Protein 49g

Creamy Mushroom & White Wine Chicken

Prep time: 36 minutes | Cook time: 26 minutes | Serves 4

- 1 tbsp butter
- 1 tbsp olive oil
- 1 pound chicken breasts, cut into chunks
- Salt and black pepper to taste
- 1 packet white onion soup mix
- 2 cups chicken broth
- ¼ cup white wine
- 15 baby Bella mushrooms, sliced
- 1 cup heavy cream
- 2 tbsp parsley, chopped

1. Add butter and olive oil in a saucepan and heat over medium heat. Season the chicken with salt and black pepper, and brown on all sides for 6 minutes in total. Put on a plate.
2. In a bowl, stir the onion soup mix with chicken broth and white wine, and add to the saucepan. Simmer for 3 minutes and add the mushrooms and chicken. Cover and simmer for another 20 minutes. Stir in heavy cream and cook on low heat for 3 minutes. Garnish with parsley to serve.

PER SERVING

Calories: 432 | Fat: 35.3g | Net Carbs: 3.2g | Protein 24.2g

Chapter 6

Beef, Lamb and Pork

Leek & Beef Bake

Prep time: 50 minutes | Cook time: 35 minutes | Serves 4

- 3 tbsp olive oil
- 1 pound beef steak racks
- 2 leeks, sliced
- Salt and black pepper, to taste
- ½ cup apple cider vinegar
- 1 tsp Italian seasoning
- 1 tbsp xylitol

1. Preheat the oven to 420 F.
2. In a bowl, mix the leeks with 2 tbsp of oil, xylitol, and vinegar, toss to coat well, and set to a baking dish. Season with Italian seasoning, black pepper and salt, and cook in the oven for 15 minutes.
3. Sprinkle pepper and salt to the beef, place into an oiled pan over medium heat, and cook for a couple of minutes. Place the beef to the baking dish with the leeks, and bake for 20 minutes.

PER SERVING

Calories: 234 | Fat: 12g | Net Carbs: 4.8g | Protein 15.5g

Kalua Pork with Cabbage

Prep time: 10 minutes | Cook time: 8 hours | Serves 2

- 1 pound boneless pork butt roast
- Pink Himalayan salt
- Freshly ground black pepper
- 1 tablespoon smoked paprika or Liquid Smoke
- ½ cup water
- ½ head cabbage, chopped

1. with the crock insert in place, preheat the slow cooker to low.
2. Generously season the pork roast with pink Himalayan salt, pepper, and smoked paprika.
3. Place the pork roast in the slow-cooker insert, and add the water.
4. Cover and cook on low for 7 hours.
5. Transfer the cooked pork roast to a plate. Put the chopped cabbage in the bottom of the slow cooker, and put the pork roast back in on top of the cabbage.
6. Cover and cook the cabbage and pork roast for 1 hour.
7. Remove the pork roast from the slow cooker and place it on a baking sheet. Use two forks to shred the pork.
8. Serve the shredded pork hot with the cooked cabbage.
9. Reserve the liquid from the slow cooker to remoisten the pork and cabbage when reheating leftovers.

PER SERVING

Calories: 550 | Total Fat: 41g | Carbs: 10g | Net Carbs: 5g | Fiber: 5g | Protein: 39g

Thyme Beef & Bacon Casserole

Prep time: 45 minutes | Cook time: 28 minutes |Serves 4

- 2 tbsp olive oil
- 2 tbsp ghee
- 1 cup pumpkin, chopped
- 1 tbsp red vinegar
- 2 cups beef stock
- 1 tbsp tomato puree
- 1 cinnamon stick
- 1 lemon peel strip
- 3 thyme sprigs, chopped
- Salt and black pepper, to taste

1. Put a saucepan over medium heat and warm oil, add in the celery, garlic and onion, and cook for 3 minutes. Stir in the beef and bacon, and cook until slightly brown. Pour in the vinegar, ghee, lemon peel strip, beef stock, tomato puree, cinnamon stick and pumpkin.
2. Cover and cook for 25 minutes. Get rid of the lemon peel and cinnamon stick. Adjust the seasoning and sprinkle with thyme to serve.

PER SERVING

Calories: 552 | Fat: 41g | Net Carbs: 4.5g | Protein 32.3g

Mexican-Inspired Beef Chili

Prep time: 45 minutes | Cook time: 30 minutes |Serves 4

- 2 tbsp olive oil
- 1 onion, chopped
- 1 tsp chipotle chili paste
- 1 garlic clove, minced
- 3 celery stalks, chopped
- 2 tbsp coconut aminos
- Salt and black pepper, to taste
- 2 tbsp cumin
- 1 tsp chopped cilantro

1. Put a pan over medium heat and warm olive oil, add in the onion, celery, garlic, beef, black pepper, and salt; cook until the meat browns.
2. Stir in the rest of the ingredients, except for cilantro and cook for 30 minutes. Sprinkle with cilantro and serve.

PER SERVING

Calories: 441 | Fat: 24.3g | Net Carbs: 3.8g | Protein 16.5g

Pork Chops with Raspberry Sauce

Prep time: 18 minutes | Cook time: 9 minutes | Serves 4

- 2 tbsp olive oil
- 2 lb pork chops
- Salt and black pepper to taste
- 2 cups raspberries
- ¼ cup water
- 1 ½ tbsp Italian herb mix
- 3 tbsp balsamic vinegar
- 2 tsp Worcestershire sauce

1. Heat oil in a skillet over medium heat, season the pork with salt and black pepper and cook for 5 minutes on each side. Put in serving plates, and reserve the pork drippings.
2. Mash raspberries with a fork in a bowl until jam-like. Pour into a saucepan, add water, and herb mix. Cook on low heat for 4 minutes. Stir in pork drippings, vinegar, and Worcestershire sauce. Simmer for 1 minute. Dish the pork chops, spoon sauce over, and serve with braised rapini.

PER SERVING

Calories: 413 | Net Carbs: 1.1g | Fat: 32.5g | Protein 26.3g

Classic Italian Bolognese Sauce

Prep time: 35 minutes | Cook time: 20 minutes | Serves 5

- pound ground beef
- garlic cloves
- 1 onion, chopped
- 1 tsp oregano
- 1 tsp sage
- 1 tsp rosemary
- 7 oz canned chopped tomatoes
- 1 tbsp olive oil

1. Heat olive oil in a saucepan. Add onion and garlic and cook for 3 minutes. Add beef and cook until browned, about 4-5 minutes.
2. Stir in the herbs and tomatoes. Cook for 15 minutes. Serve with zoodles.

PER SERVING

Calories: 318 | Fat: 20g | Net Carbs: 5.9g | Protein: 26g

Citrus Pork with Sauteed Cabbage & Tomatoes

Prep time: 27 minutes | Cook time: 13 minutes | Serves 4

- 3 tbsp olive oil
- 2 tbsp lemon juice
- 1 garlic clove, pureed
- 4 pork loin chops
- 1/3 head cabbage, shredded
- 1 tomato, chopped
- 1 tbsp white wine
- Salt and black pepper to taste
- ¼ tsp cumin
- ¼ tsp ground nutmeg
- 1 tbsp parsley

1. In a bowl, mix the lemon juice, garlic, salt, pepper and olive oil. Brush the pork with the mixture.
2. Preheat grill to high heat. Grill the pork for 2-3 minutes on each side until cooked through.
3. Drizzle with white wine, sprinkle with cumin, nutmeg, salt and pepper. Add in the tomatoes, cook for another 5 minutes, stirring occasionally. Ladle the sautéed cabbage to the side of the chops and serve sprinkled with parsley.

PER SERVING

Calories: 565 | Fat: 36.7g | Net Carbs: 6.1g | Protein 43g

Green Chimichurri Sauce with Pork Steaks

Prep time: 64 minutes | Cook time: 5 minutes | Serves 4

- 1 garlic clove, minced
- ½ tsp white wine vinegar
- 2 tbsp parsley leaves, chopped
- 2 tbsp cilantro leaves, chopped
- 2 tbsp extra-virgin olive oil
- 16 oz pork loin steaks
- Salt and black pepper to season
- 2 tbsp sesame oil

1. To make the sauce: in a bowl, mix the parsley, cilantro and garlic. Add the vinegar, extra-virgin olive oil, and salt, and combine well. Preheat a grill pan over medium heat.
2. Rub the pork with sesame oil, and season with salt and pepper. Grill the meat for 4-5 minutes on each side until no longer pink in the center. Put the pork on a serving plate and spoon chimichurri sauce over, to serve.

PER SERVING

Calories: 452 | Fat: 33.6g | Net Carbs: 2.3g | Protein 32.8g

Grilled Sirloin Steak with Sauce Diane

Prep time: 25 minutes | Cook time: 13 minutes | Serves 6

- Sirloin Steak
- 1 ½ lb sirloin steak
- Salt and black pepper to taste
- 1 tsp olive oil
- Sauce Diane
- 1 tbsp olive oil
- 1 clove garlic, minced
- 1 cup sliced porcini mushrooms
- 1 small onion, finely diced
- 2 tbsp butter
- 1 tbsp Dijon mustard
- 2 tbsp Worcestershire sauce
- ¼ cup whiskey
- 2 cups double cream
- Salt and black pepper to taste

1. Put a grill pan over high heat and as it heats, brush the steak with oil, sprinkle with salt and pepper, and rub the seasoning into the meat with your hands. Cook the steak in the pan for 4 minutes on each side for medium rare and transfer to a chopping board to rest for 4 minutes before slicing. Reserve the juice.
2. Heat the oil in a frying pan over medium heat and sauté the onion for 3 minutes. Add the butter, garlic, and mushrooms, and cook for 2 minutes.
3. Add the Worcestershire sauce, the reserved juice, and mustard. Stir and cook for 1 minute. Pour in the whiskey and cook further 1 minute until the sauce reduces by half. Swirl the pan and add the cream. Let it simmer to thicken for about 3 minutes. Adjust the taste with salt and pepper. Spoon the sauce over the steaks slices and serve with celeriac mash.

PER SERVING

Calories: 434 | Fat: 17g | Net Carbs: 2.9g | Protein: 36g

Cauli Rice with Vegetables and Beef Steak

Prep time: 25 minutes | Cook time: 10 minutes | Serves 4

- 2 cups cauli rice
- 3 cups mixed vegetables
- 3 tbsp ghee
- 1 lb beef skirt steak
- Salt and black pepper to taste
- 4 fresh eggs
- Hot sauce (sugar-free) for topping

1. Mix the cauliflower rice with mixed vegetables in a bowl, sprinkle with a little water, and steam in the microwave for 1 minute to tender. Share into 4 serving bowls.
2. Melt the ghee in a skillet, season the beef with salt and pepper, and brown in the ghee for 5 minutes on each side. Use a perforated spoon to ladle the meat onto the vegetables.
3. Wipe out the skillet and return to medium heat, crack in an egg, season 3 eggs. Add to the other bowls. Drizzle the beef bowl with hot sauce, and serve.

PER SERVING

Calories: 320 | Net Carbs: 4g | Fat: 26g | Protein 15g

Mind-Blowing Burgers

Prep time: 15 minutes | Cook time: 15 minutes | Serves 6

Burger Patties
- 1 pound (455 g) ground beef (20% to 30% fat)
- 1 heaping tablespoon prepared horseradish
- 1½ teaspoons ground mustard
- ¼ teaspoon finely ground gray sea salt
- ¼ teaspoon ground black pepper

"Buns"
- 1 medium eggplant, sliced into 3/8-inch (1-cm) thick rounds (about 10½ ounces/300 g edible portion)
- 3 tablespoons refined avocado oil or melted tallow

Fixings
- 1 large Hass avocado, peeled, pitted, and mashed (about 6 ounces/170 g flesh)
- 6 tablespoons (90 ml) mayonnaise, homemade (here) or store-bought, or Kickin' Ketchup
- 6 small lettuce leaves

1. Make the burgers: Preheat the oven to 375°F (190°C) and line a rimmed baking sheet with parchment paper or a silicone baking mat.
2. Place the burger patty ingredients in a medium-sized bowl. Mix with your hands until fully combined.
3. Divide the meat mixture into 6 equal portions, then shape into ½-inch (1.25-cm) thick patties.
4. Arrange the patties on the prepared baking sheet, leaving at least 1 inch (2.5 cm) of space between patties. Transfer to the oven and cook for 10 to 15 minutes, until the desired doneness is achieved. For medium-rare, cook for 10 minutes; for medium, 12 minutes; for medium-well, 14 minutes; and for well-done, 15 minutes.
5. Meanwhile, make the "buns": Place a large frying pan over medium-high heat. While the pan is heating up, place the eggplant slices in a bowl and drizzle them with avocado oil, turning them to ensure that the slices are evenly coated.
6. Transfer the coated eggplant slices to the frying pan. Sear for up to 1 minute per side, only until lightly golden. Repeat with the remaining slices, moving them to a cooling rack when done.
7. Assemble the burgers: Place an eggplant slice on a serving plate, top with a 1-ounce (28-g) scoop of mashed avocado, then place a patty on top, followed by a tablespoon of mayonnaise, a tablespoon of ketchup, a leaf of romaine, and a second eggplant slice. Repeat with the remaining fixings.

PER SERVING

Calories: 493 | Fat: 41.4g | Carbs: 8.3g | Dietary Fiber: 4.4g | Net Carbs: 3.9g | Sugars: 3.3g | Protein: 21.7g

Blue Cheese Pork Chops

Prep time: 5 minutes | Cook time: 10 minutes | Serves 2

- 2 boneless pork chops
- Pink Himalayan salt
- Freshly ground black pepper
- 2 tablespoons butter
- ⅓ cup blue cheese crumbles
- ⅓ cup heavy (whipping) cream
- ⅓ cup sour cream

1. Pat the pork chops dry, and season with pink Himalayan salt and pepper.
2. In a medium skillet over medium heat, melt the butter. When the butter melts and is very hot, add the pork chops and sear on each side for 3 minutes.
3. Transfer the pork chops to a plate and let rest for 3 to 5 minutes.
4. In a medium saucepan over medium heat, melt the blue cheese crumbles, stirring frequently so they don't burn.
5. Add the cream and the sour cream to the pan with the blue cheese. Let simmer for a few minutes, stirring occasionally.
6. For an extra kick of flavor in the sauce, pour the pork-chop pan juice into the cheese mixture and stir. Let simmer while the pork chops are resting.
7. Put the pork chops on two plates, pour the blue cheese sauce over the top of each, and serve.

PER SERVING

Calories: 669 | Total Fat: 34g | Carbs: 4g | Net Carbs: 4g | Fiber: 0g | Protein: 41g

Chili-Stuffed Avocados

Prep time: 10 minutes | Cook time: 30 minutes | Serves 8

- 2 tablespoons tallow or bacon grease
- 1 pound (455 g) ground beef (20% to 30% fat)
- 1 (14½-ounce/408-g/428-ml) can whole tomatoes with juices
- 1½ tablespoons chili powder
- 2 small cloves garlic, minced
- 2 teaspoons paprika
- ¾ teaspoon finely ground gray sea salt
- ¼ teaspoon ground cinnamon
- 2 tablespoons finely chopped fresh parsley
- 4 large Hass avocados, sliced in half, pits removed (leave skin on), for serving

1. Place the tallow into a large saucepan. Melt on medium heat before adding the ground beef. Cook until beef is no longer pink, 7 to 8 minutes, stirring often to break the meat up into small clumps.
2. Add the tomatoes, chili powder, garlic, paprika, salt, and cinnamon. Cover and bring to a boil on high heat. Once boiling, reduce the heat to medium-low and simmer for 20 to 25 minutes, with the cover slightly askew to let steam out.
3. Once thickened, remove from the heat and stir in the chopped parsley.

PER SERVING

Calories: 385 | Fat: 30.5g | Carbs: 10.3g | Dietary Fiber: 7g | Net Carbs: 3.3g | Sugars: 1.7g | Protein: 17.2g

Ground Beef Stew with Majoram & Basil

Prep time: 30 minutes | Cook time: 26 minutes | Serves 4

- 2 tbsp olive oil
- ¼ cup red wine
- 1 pound ground beef
- 1 onion, chopped
- 14 ounces canned diced tomatoes
- 1 tbsp dried basil
- 1 tbsp dried marjoram
- Salt and black pepper, to taste
- 2 carrots, sliced
- 2 celery stalks, chopped
- 1 cup vegetable broth

1. Put a pan over medium heat, add in the olive oil, onion, carrots, celery, and garlic, and sauté for 5 minutes. Place in the beef and cook for 6 minutes.
2. Stir in the tomatoes, carrots, red wine, vegetable broth, black pepper, marjoram, basil, and salt, and simmer for 15 minutes. Serve and enjoy!

PER SERVING

Calories: 274 | Fat: 14.3g | Net Carbs: 6.2g | Protein 29.5g

Beef Roast with Serrano Pepper Gravy

Prep time: 1 hour 25 minutes | Cook time: 1 hour | Serves 4

- 2 pounds beef roast
- 1 cup mushrooms, sliced
- 1½ cups beef stock
- 1 ounce onion soup mix
- ½ cup basil dressing
- 2 serrano peppers, shredded

1. Preheat the oven to 350 F. In a bowl, combine the stock with the basil dressing and onion soup mixture. Place the beef roast in a pan, stir in the stock mixture, mushrooms, and serrano peppers.
2. Bake for 1 hour. Allow the roast to cool, then slice, and serve alongside a topping of the gravy.

PER SERVING

Calories: 722 | Fat: 51g | Net Carbs: 5.1g | Protein 71g

Pork Burgers with Sriracha Mayo

Prep time: 10 minutes | Cook time: 10 minutes | Serves 2

- 12 ounces ground pork
- Pink Himalayan salt
- Freshly ground black pepper
- 1 tablespoon ghee
- 1 tablespoon Sriracha sauce
- 2 tablespoons mayonnaise

1. In a large bowl, mix to combine the ground pork with the scallions and sesame oil, and season with pink Himalayan salt and pepper. Form the pork mixture into 2 patties. Create an imprint with your thumb in the middle of each burger so the pork will heat evenly.
2. In a large skillet over medium-high heat, heat the ghee. When the ghee has melted and is very hot, add the burger patties and cook for 4 minutes on each side.
3. Meanwhile, in a small bowl, mix the Sriracha sauce and mayonnaise.
4. Transfer the burgers to a plate and let rest for at least 5 minutes.
5. Top the burgers with the Sriracha mayonnaise and serve.

PER SERVING

Calories: 575 | Total Fat: 49g | Carbs: 2g | Net Carbs: 1g | Fiber: 1g | Protein: 31g

Beef Skewers with Ranch Dressing

Prep time: 25 minutes | Cook time: 6 minutes | Serves 4

- 1 lb sirloin steak, boneless, cubed
- ¼ cup ranch dressing, divided
- Chopped scallions to garnish

1. Preheat the grill on medium heat to 400°F and thread the beef cubes on the skewers, about 4 to 5 cubes per skewer. Brush half of the ranch dressing on the skewers (all around) and place them on the grill grate to cook for 6 minutes. Turn the skewers once and cook further for 6 minutes.
2. Brush the remaining ranch dressing on the meat and cook them for 1 more minute on each side. Plate, garnish with the scallions, and serve with a mixed veggie salad, and extra ranch dressing.

PER SERVING

Calories: 230 | Fat: 14g | Net Carbs: 3g | Protein: 21g

Steak with Tallow Herb Butter

Prep time: 10 minutes | Cook time: 10 minutes | Serves 4

- 13 ounces (370 g) boneless sirloin steak (aka strip steak or beef strip loin steak), about 1 inch (2.5 cm) thick
- ¾ teaspoon ground black pepper
- ¼ teaspoon garlic powder
- ¼ teaspoon finely ground gray sea salt

Tallow Herb Butter
- ¼ cup (52 g) tallow
- 1 sprig fresh thyme
- 1 sprig fresh rosemary
- 1 sprig fresh parsley
- 1 sprig fresh sage

1. Remove the steak from the fridge and place on a clean plate. Sprinkle the pepper, garlic powder, and salt over both sides of the steak. Wet your hands and rub the spices into the steak, on both sides, until a paste forms. If you require a bit more water, wet your hands again. Allow the coated steak to sit for 30 minutes.
2. Meanwhile, make the tallow herb butter: Melt the tallow in a small saucepan on medium heat. Add the remaining ingredients, cover, and reduce the heat to low. Simmer for 10 minutes. Once complete, strain the herbs and transfer the tallow herb butter back to the saucepan. Place the saucepan at the back of the stovetop, just to keep warm.
3. Place the steak in the pan and sear for 30 seconds without moving it, then flip the steak over and sear the other side for 30 seconds. (Remember to use an oven mitt when touching the pan handle.)
4. Once seared, transfer the pan with the steak to the oven. Broil for 2 to 4 minutes, take the pan out of the oven and flip it, then return it to the oven to broil for another 2 to 4 minutes, depending on your desired doneness. (For medium-rare, cook for a total of 4 minutes; for medium, 5 minutes; for medium-well, 6 minutes; and for well-done, 8 minutes.)
5. Remove the pan from the oven and allow the steak to cool for 5 minutes.
6. Transfer to a cutting board to slice, divide among 4 plates, and drizzle with the tallow herb butter.

PER SERVING

Calories: 304 | Fat: 24.4g | Carbs: 0.5g | Dietary Fiber: 0g | Net Carbs: 0.5g | Sugars: 0g | Protein: 20.5g

Traditional Bolognese Sauce with Zoodles

Prep time: 35 minutes | Cook time: 27 minutes |Serves 4

- 2 cups zoodles
- 1 pound ground beef
- 2 garlic cloves
- 1 onion, chopped
- 1 tsp oregano
- 1 tsp sage
- 1 tsp rosemary
- 7 oz canned chopped tomatoes
- 2 tbsp olive oil

1. Cook the zoodles in warm olive oil over medium heat for 3-4 minutes and remove to a serving plate. To the same pan, add onion and garlic and cook for 3 minutes. Add beef and cook until browned, about 4-5 minutes.
2. Stir in the herbs and tomatoes. Cook for 15 minutes and serve over the zoodles.

PER SERVING

Calories: 336 | Fat: 21g | Net Carbs: 7.3g | Protein 29g

Slow-Cooker Barbecue Ribs

Prep time: 10 minutes | Cook time: 4 hours | Serves 2

- 1 pound pork ribs
- Pink Himalayan salt
- Freshly ground black pepper
- 1 (1.25-ounce) package dry rib-seasoning rub
- ½ cup sugar-free barbecue sauce

1. with the crock insert in place, preheat the slow cooker to high.
2. Generously season the pork ribs with pink Himalayan salt, pepper, and dry rib-seasoning rub.
3. Stand the ribs up along the walls of the slow-cooker insert, with the bonier side facing inward.
4. Pour the barbecue sauce on both sides of the ribs, using just enough to coat.
5. Cover, cook for 4 hours, and serve.

PER SERVING

Calories: 956 | Total Fat: 72g | Carbs: 5g | Net Carbs: 5g | Fiber: 0g | Protein: 68g

Cabbage & Sausage with Bacon

Prep time: 10 minutes | Cook time:25 minutes |Serves 4

- 6 strips bacon (about 6 oz/170 g), diced
- 1 small red onion, diced
- 4 cloves garlic, minced
- 1 small head green cabbage (about 1⅓ lbs/600 g), cored and thinly sliced
- 12 ounces (340 g) Mexican-style fresh (raw) chorizo, thinly sliced
- ¼ cup (60 ml) beef bone broth

1. Place the bacon, onion, and garlic in a large frying pan and sauté over medium heat until the bacon begins to crisp, about 10 minutes.
2. Remove the lid, divide among 4 dinner plates, and enjoy!

PER SERVING

Calories: 312 | Net Carbs:2g | Fat: 22.5g | Protein 16.3g

Bombay Sloppy Jolenes

Prep time: 15 minutes | Cook time: 40 minutes | Serves 8

- ¼ cup (60 ml) plus 1½ teaspoons refined avocado oil or melted tallow
- ¼ cup (40 g) finely diced red onions
- 1 (2 by 1-in/5 by 2.5-cm) piece fresh ginger root, minced
- 2 small cloves garlic, minced
- 1 teaspoon cumin seeds
- 1⅔ cups (390 ml) sugar-free tomato sauce
- ¾ cup (180 ml) water
- 1 to 2 whole dried chilis, crushed
- 2 teaspoons Curry Powder
- 1 teaspoon finely ground gray sea salt
- ½ teaspoon paprika
- ⅓ cup (57 g) raw macadamia nut halves
- ½ cup (120 ml) full-fat coconut milk
- 1 tablespoon apple cider vinegar
- ¼ cup (15 g) fresh cilantro leaves, chopped, plus more for garnish

1. In a large saucepan on medium heat, place ¼ cup (60 ml) of the oil, onion, ginger, garlic, and cumin seeds. Cook for 2 to 3 minutes, until fragrant.
2. Add the ground beef and cook until no longer pink, about 8 minutes, stirring often to break the meat up into small clumps.
3. Add the tomatoes, water, crushed chilis, curry powder, salt, and paprika and stir. Cover partially, letting steam escape. Bring to a boil, reduce the heat to medium-low and simmer for 25 minutes.
4. Using a spoon, transfer the Sloppy Jolene mixture to the endive leaves. Garnish with additional cilantro, if desired.

PER SERVING

Calories: 338 | Fat: 26.7g |Carbs: 8.1g | Dietary Fiber: 2.8g | Net Carbs: 5.3g | Sugars: 2.8g | Protein: 16.4g

Cheesy Meatballs & Noodles

Prep time: 10 minutes | Cook time:20 minutes |Serves 6

Meatballs:
- 1 pound (455 g) ground turkey
- 1 pound (455 g) ground pork
- ½ cup (70 g) shredded mozzarella cheese (dairy-free or regular)
- 2 tablespoons hot sauce
- 2 teaspoons dried oregano leaves
- 1½ teaspoons dried basil
- 1¼ teaspoons garlic powder
- 1 teaspoon onion powder
- ¾ teaspoon finely ground sea salt
- ½ teaspoon dried rosemary leaves
- 3 tablespoons avocado oil or coconut oil
- 4 medium zucchinis, spiral sliced
- 1 tablespoon lemon juice

1. Place the turkey, pork, cheese, hot sauce, oregano, basil, garlic powder, onion powder, salt, and rosemary in a large mixing bowl and combine with your hands until fully incorporated.
2. Heat the oil in a large frying pan over medium heat. While the oil is heating, form the meatballs: Take 3 tablespoons of the meat mixture, roll it into a ball between your palms, and place it in the frying pan. Repeat with the remaining meat mixture, placing the meatballs as close together as possible so that they all fit in the pan at one time. You should get about 18 meatballs.
3. Cover the pan and cook the meatballs for 15 minutes, or until fully cooked.
4. Divide the noodles and meatballs among 6 dinner plates and dig in.

PER SERVING

Calories: 595 | Fat: 45.2 g |Carbs: 3.6 g | Dietary Fiber: 1 g | Net Carbs: 2.6 g | Sugars: 0.9 g | Protein: 43.8 g

Chapter 7

Fish and Seafood

Homemade Lobster Salad Rolls

Prep time: 1 hour 10 minutes | Cook time: 20 minutes | Serves 4

- 5 cups cauliflower florets
- 1/3 cup celery, diced
- 2 cups large shrimp, cooked
- 1 tbsp bill, chopped
- ½ cup mayonnaise
- 1 tsp apple cider vinegar
- ¼ tsp celery seeds
- 2 tbsp lemon juice
- 2 tsp swerve sweetener
- Salt and black pepper to taste

1. Combine cauliflower, celery, shrimp, and dill in a large bowl. Whisk mayonnaise, vinegar, celery seeds, sweetener, and lemon juice in another bowl.
2. Season with salt. Pour the dressing over the salad, and gently toss to combine. Serve cold.

PER SERVING

Calories: 182 | Net Carbs: 2g | Fat: 15g | Protein 12g

Greek Salad with Grilled Salmon

Prep time: 15 minutes | Cook time: 8 minutes | Serves 4

Salad
- 2 medium heads romaine lettuce, chopped
- ½ medium cucumber, chopped
- ¾ cup cherry tomatoes, halved
- ¾ cup crumbled feta cheese
- ½ cup pitted Kalamata olives
- ½ cup thinly sliced red onions
- 1 teaspoon dried ground oregano
- Pinch of salt
- Pinch of ground black pepper

Dressing
- ¼ cup extra-virgin olive oil
- ¼ cup red wine vinegar
- 1 large clove garlic, minced
- 2 teaspoons onion powder
- 2 teaspoons dried ground oregano
- Salt and pepper
- Salmon
- 4 (6-ounce) skin-on salmon fillets
- 1 tablespoon extra-virgin olive oil
- Salt and pepper
- 1 tablespoon avocado oil or other cooking oil of choice, for the grill grates Fresh dill, for garnish (optional)

1. In a large bowl, combine all the salad ingredients and toss. Divide the salad among 4 bowls and set aside.
2. Make the dressing: Place the olive oil, vinegar, garlic, oregano, and onion powder in a bowl and whisk to combine. Season with salt and pepper to taste and set aside.
3. Rinse the salmon and pat dry. Brush the salmon with the olive oil and season with salt and pepper.
4. Preheat a grill to medium-high heat, then brush the hot grill grates with the avocado oil.
5. Place the salmon skin side up on the grill, close the grill lid, and cook for 2 minutes. Flip the salmon and cook skin side down for 5 to 6 minutes, until the internal temperature reaches 145°F.
6. Allow the salmon to rest for a few minutes, then place a fillet on top of each salad. Whisk the salad dressing again and drizzle it over the salads.
7. Garnish with fresh dill, if desired, and enjoy!

PER SERVING

Calories: 588 | Fat: 41.7 g | Protein: 42 g | Total Carbs: 10.3 g | Net Carbs: 7.8 g

Parmesan-Crusted Salmon Bake with Asparagus

Prep time: 15 minutes | Cook time: 15 minutes | Serves 4

- 1½ to 2 pounds asparagus (6 to 8 spears per serving)
- 3 tablespoons coconut oil, melted but not hot
- 1 teaspoon garlic powder
- ⅓ cup grated Parmesan cheese
- ¼ cup plus 2 tablespoons mayonnaise
- 1 clove garlic, pressed
- 4 salmon fillets (about 6 ounces each), rinsed and patted dry Finely chopped fresh dill or dill sprigs, for garnish (optional) 1 lemon, sliced, for serving (optional)

1. Preheat the oven to 350°F.
2. Rinse the asparagus and trim or snap off the tough end of each spear.
3. Place the asparagus, coconut oil, and garlic powder in a zip-top plastic bag, seal, and shake lightly to coat the asparagus.
4. In a bowl, mix the Parmesan cheese, mayonnaise, and pressed garlic.
5. Lay out 4 rectangular pieces of parchment paper, large enough to fit the asparagus and fish with plenty of paper remaining on the sides and ends to fold into packets and seal. Divide the seasoned asparagus evenly among the sheets of parchment.
6. Place the fillets on top of the asparagus, skin side down. Top the salmon with the mayonnaise mixture.
7. Fold the parchment paper over the fish and seal on all sides. The packet should look like a calzone.
8. Place the packets on a rimmed baking sheet and bake for 12 to 15
9. minutes, until the internal temperature of the salmon reaches 145°F.
10. Garnish with fresh dill and lemon slices, if desired.

PER SERVING

Calories: 477 | Fat: 33.3 g | Protein: 38.5 g | Total Carbs: 7.25 g | Net Carbs: 3.8 g

Shrimp Fry

Prep time: 5 minutes | Cook time: 20 minutes | Serves 4

- ¼ cup (55 g) coconut oil
- 1 pound (455 g) medium shrimp, peeled, deveined, and tails removed
- 12 ounces (340 g) smoked sausage (chicken, pork, beef—anything goes), cubed
- 5 asparagus spears, woody ends snapped off, thinly sliced
- 4 ounces (115 g) cremini mushrooms, sliced
- 1 medium zucchini, cubed
- 1 tablespoon paprika
- 2 teaspoons garlic powder
- 1 teaspoon onion powder
- 1 teaspoon dried thyme leaves
- ½ teaspoon finely ground sea salt
- ¼ teaspoon ground black pepper
- Pinch of cayenne pepper (optional)
- Handful of fresh parsley leaves, chopped, for serving

1. Melt the oil in a large frying pan over medium heat.
2. Add the remaining ingredients, except the parsley. Toss to coat in the oil, then cover and cook for 15 to 20 minutes, until the asparagus is tender and the shrimp has turned pink.
3. Divide the mixture among 4 serving plates, sprinkle with parsley, and serve.

PER SERVING

Calories: 574 | Fat: 40.1 g | Carbs: 8.4 g | Dietary Fiber: 2.3 g | Net Carbs: 6.1 g | Sugars: 2.6 g | Protein: 45 g

Niçoise Salad with Seared Tuna

Prep time: 10 minutes | Cook time: 8 minutes | Serves 4

- 1 tablespoon sugar-free mayonnaise
- 1 teaspoon Dijon mustard
- ½ teaspoon kosher salt
- ¼ teaspoon ground black pepper
- 1 pound ahi tuna steaks
- 1 tablespoon avocado oil or other light-tasting oil, for the pan
- 2 medium heads red or green leaf lettuce, leaves washed and dried
- 8 hard-boiled eggs, peeled and quartered
- 2 cups cooked cauliflower florets
- 2 cups blanched green beans
- 2 large tomatoes, cut into wedges
- For the Dijon vinaigrette:
- ¼ cup extra-virgin olive oil
- ¼ cup red wine vinegar
- ¼ cup sugar-free mayonnaise
- 1 tablespoon Dijon mustard
- ¼ teaspoon kosher salt
- ⅛ teaspoon ground black pepper

1. Combine the mayonnaise, mustard, salt, and pepper in a small bowl. Coat the tuna steaks on all sides with the mixture.
2. Heat the oil in a medium-sized nonstick pan over medium-high heat. Add the tuna steaks and sear for about 2 minutes per side for rare or 4 minutes per side to cook them through. Remove from the pan and set aside.
3. Place the lettuce leaves on a serving platter or divide them among 4 individual serving plates. Arrange the eggs, cauliflower, green beans, and tomato wedges around the outer edges on top of the lettuce.
4. Place the tuna steaks, whole or cut into pieces, in the center of the platter or plates.
5. In a medium-sized bowl, whisk together the vinaigrette ingredients. Drizzle over the salad just before serving.

PER SERVING

Calories: 546 | Fat: 37g | Protein: 16g | Carbs: 12g | Fiber: 6g | Net Carbs: 6g

Baked Cod with Parmesan and Almonds

Prep time: 40 minutes | Cook time: 30 minutes |Serves 2

- 4 cod fillets
- 1 cup Brussels sprouts
- 1 tbsp butter, melted
- Salt and black pepper to taste
- 1 cup crème fraiche
- 2 tbsp Parmesan cheese, grated
- 2 tbsp shaved almonds

1. Toss the fish fillets and Brussels sprouts in butter with salt and black pepper to taste. Spread in a greased baking dish.
2. Mix crème fraiche with Parmesan cheese; pour and smear the cream on the fish. Bake in the oven for 25 minutes at 400 F, take the dish out, sprinkle with almonds and bake for 5 minutes. Best served hot.

PER SERVING

Calories: 560 | Fat: 44.7g | Net Carbs: 5.4g | Protein 25.3g

Mediterranean-Style Halibut Fillets

Prep time: 5 minutes | Cook time: 35 minutes |Serves 4

- 1 ½ pounds halibut fillets
- 2 tablespoons olive oil
- 2 tablespoons fresh lemon juice
- 1 tablespoon Greek seasoning blend
- 1/2 cup Kalamata olives, pitted and sliced

1. Start by preheating your oven to 380 degrees F.
2. Toss the halibut fillets with the olive oil, fresh lemon juice, and Greek seasoning blend. Arrange the halibut fillets in a baking pan and cover with foil.
3. Bake approximately 30 minutes, flipping once or twice.
4. Garnish with Kalamata olives and serve warm. Bon appétit!

PER SERVING

Calories: 397 | Fat: 32.1g | Carbs: 1.5g | Protein: 24.6g | Fiber: 0.6

Spicy Tuna Cakes

Prep time: 10 minutes | Cook time: 10 minutes | Makes 12 cakes

- 3 tablespoons sugar-free mayonnaise
- 1 tablespoon Sriracha sauce
- 1 teaspoon wheat-free soy sauce
- 1 teaspoon coconut flour
- 1 pound fresh tuna, cut into ½-inch cubes
- 2 tablespoons white sesame seeds
- 1 tablespoon black sesame seeds
- 2 tablespoons avocado oil or other light-tasting oil, for the pan

1. In a mixing bowl, whisk together the mayonnaise, Sriracha, soy sauce, and flour until smooth. Add the tuna and stir to combine.
2. Combine the white and black sesame seeds and spread on a small plate.
3. Heat the oil in a medium-sized nonstick sauté pan over medium heat. Cook the cakes in batches, 1 to 2 minutes per side, until golden brown. Serve warm.

PER SERVING

Calories: 299 | Fat: 19g | Protein: 27g | Carbs: 2g | Fiber: 1g | Net Carbs: 1g

The Best Sardine Burgers Ever

Prep time: 5 minutes | Cook time: 15 minutes |Serves 3

- 2 (5.5-ounces) canned sardines, drained
- 3 tablespoons flaxseed meal
- 1 tablespoon dry Italian seasoning blend
- 1 teaspoon fresh garlic, peeled and minced
- 1/2 onion, chopped
- 1/2 teaspoon celery salt
- Freshly ground black pepper, to taste
- 1/2 teaspoon smoked paprika
- 2 tablespoons butter

1. In a mixing dish, thoroughly combine the sardines with the cheese, egg, flaxseed meal, dry Italian seasoning blend, garlic, and onion.
2. Season with the celery salt, black pepper, and smoked paprika. Form the mixture into six equal patties.
3. Melt the butter in a frying pan over a moderate flame. Once hot, fry the fish burgers for 4 to 6 minutes on each side. Serve garnished with fresh lemon slices. Bon appétit!

PER SERVING

Calories: 267 | Fat: 21.3g | Carbs: 6.1g | Protein: 13.5g | Fiber: 3.3g

Low-Carb Crab Cakes

Prep time: 15 minutes | Cook time: 10 minutes |Serves 1

- 1 large egg
- ¼ cup mayonnaise
- 1 green onion, chopped, plus extra for garnish (optional) 1 teaspoon Old Bay seasoning
- 1 tablespoon Dijon mustard
- 1 tablespoon chopped fresh parsley
- 1½ teaspoons fresh lemon juice
- 1 pound fresh lump crabmeat
- ¼ cup golden flaxseed meal
- 2 to 3 tablespoons avocado oil, for frying
- Spring mix greens or arugula, for serving (optional)
- Lemon wedges, for serving (optional)

1. In a large mixing bowl, combine the egg and mayonnaise and whisk until smooth. Add the green onion, Old Bay seasoning, mustard, parsley, and lemon juice and mix well.
2. Sort through the crabmeat to ensure that no shells remain in the meat.
3. Then add the crabmeat to the bowl with the egg mixture and gently mix with a spoon until well blended. Be sure to mix gently so that you don't break up the crabmeat too much.
4. Gently fold in the flaxseed meal.
5. Refrigerate the mixture for 20 to 30 minutes, then use your hands to form it into four 4-ounce patties.
6. Heat the avocado oil in a large skillet over medium-high heat. When hot, add the crab cakes and pan-fry for 4 to 5 minutes on each side, until golden brown and warm throughout.
7. Serve immediately. If desired, serve each crab cake over a bed of spring mix or arugula with lemon wedges on the side and garnished with extra green onions.

PER SERVING

Calories: 331 | Fat: 22 g | Protein: 28 g | Total Carbs: 3.8 g | Net Carbs: 1.75 g

Fresh Tilapia Omelet with Goat Cheese

Prep time: 10 minutes | Cook time: 20 minutes |Serves 4

- 2 tablespoons olive oil
- 1/2 cup leeks, sliced
- 1 pound tilapia fillets
- 1 red chili pepper, deseeded and sliced
- Sea salt and ground black pepper, to taste
- 1/2 teaspoon garlic powder
- 1/2 teaspoon fennel seeds
- 1 cup milk
- 4 ounces cream cheese
- 8 medium-sized eggs
- 1 cup goat cheese, crumbled

1. Heat 1 tablespoon of the olive oil in a cast-iron skillet over moderate heat. Once hot, sweat the leeks for 4 to 5 minutes, stirring periodically.
2. Then, add in the tilapia fish and cook for 5 minutes more until flesh flakes apart easily; flake the fish using a fork and reserve.
3. Add in the chili pepper, salt, black pepper, garlic powder, and fennel seeds; stir to combine.
4. When the eggs are set, spoon the fish mixture over one side, add the goat cheese and fold your omelet over the filling. Heat off.
5. Cover and let stand for 2 minutes in the residual heat until the cheese has melted. Bon appétit!

PER SERVING

Calories: 558 | Fat: 38g | Carbs: 6.5g | Protein: 45.5g | Fiber: 0.2g

Crab Tacos

Prep time: 5 minutes | Cook time: 5 minutes | Serves 4

- 1 cup (230 g) cooked crab leg meat
- 2 small tomatoes, diced
- ⅓ cup (55 g) diced radishes
- Juice of 1 lime
- 3 tablespoons extra-virgin olive oil
- 3 tablespoons finely chopped green bell pepper
- 2 tablespoons finely chopped yellow bell pepper
- 2 tablespoons finely chopped fresh cilantro, plus more for garnish
- 2 tablespoons Sriracha sauce
- 1 tablespoon finely chopped fresh mint
- ¼ teaspoon finely ground gray sea salt
- 8 Bendy Tortillas (here), for serving

1. Place all the ingredients except the tortillas in a large bowl. Toss to combine.
2. Divide the crab mixture evenly among the 8 tortillas. Garnish with additional cilantro, if using, and serve.

PER 2 TACOS

Calories: 297 | Fat: 19.5g | Carbs: 5.5g | Dietary Fiber: 1.1g | Net Carbs: 4.4g | Sugars: 3.4g | Protein: 24.9g

Smoked Salmon Stacks

Prep time: 15 minutes | Cook time: 15 minutes | Serves 4

- 8 ounces cold-smoked salmon (lox style)
- 1 cup diced cucumbers
- 1 tablespoon minced red onions
- 1 teaspoon granulated erythritol
- 1 teaspoon white vinegar
- 1 to 2 large ripe Hass avocados, halved and pitted
- 8 cups spring greens
- 8 tablespoons Creamy Lemon Caper Dressing

1. Chop the salmon into ½-inch pieces.
2. Combine the cucumbers, onions, sweetener, and vinegar in a small bowl.
3. Remove the flesh from the avocados and chop into ½-inch pieces.
4. Assemble the stacks: Spread out 2 cups of spring greens on a salad plate. Pack one-quarter of the chopped salmon into a 4-inch ramekin or dish. Top the salmon with one-quarter of the cucumber-onion mixture, then one-quarter of the chopped avocados. Press the stack down gently to compact the layers but do not mash them out of shape. Carefully turn the ramekin over on the salad greens to unmold the stack.
5. Repeat Step 4 until you have four complete stacks. Drizzle 2 tablespoons of the dressing over each stack and serve.

PER SERVING

Calories: 248 | Fat: 21g | Protein: 12g | Carbs: 5g | Fiber: 3g | Net Carbs: 2g

Sea Bass with Dijon Butter Sauce

Prep time: 5 minutes | Cook time: 20 minutes | Serves 3

- 2 tablespoons olive oil
- 2 sea bass fillets
- 1/4 teaspoon red pepper flakes, crushed
- Sea salt, to taste
- 1/3 teaspoon mixed peppercorns, crushed
- 3 tablespoons butter
- 1 tablespoon Dijon mustard
- 2 cloves garlic, minced
- 1 tablespoon fresh lime juice

1. Heat the olive oil in a skillet over medium-high heat.
2. Pat dry the sea bass fillets with paper towels. Now pan-fry the fish fillets for about 4 minutes on each side until flesh flakes easily and it is nearly opaque.
3. Season your fish with red pepper, salt, and mixed peppercorns.
4. To make the sauce, melt the 3 tablespoons of butter in a saucepan over low heat; stir in the Dijon mustard, garlic, and lime juice. Let it simmer for 2 minutes.
5. To serve, spoon the Dijon butter sauce over the fish fillets. Bon appétit!

PER SERVING

Calories: 314 | Fat: 23.2g | Carbs: 1.4g | Protein: 24.2g | Fiber: 0.3g

Crispy Salmon Steaks with Sweet Cabbage

Prep time: 10 minutes | Cook time: 40 minutes | Serves 4

- Sweet Cabbage
- ¼ cup (60 ml) refined avocado oil or macadamia nut oil
- ⅓ cup (55 g) sliced red onions
- 4 cups (470 g) sliced red cabbage
- ⅓ cup (80 ml) red wine, such as Pinot Noir, Merlot, or Cabernet Sauvignon
- ¼ cup (60 ml) chicken bone broth
- 1 tablespoon balsamic vinegar
- ½ teaspoon finely ground gray sea salt
- ¼ teaspoon ground black pepper

Salmon
- 4 salmon steaks (6 ounces/170 g each)
- 3 tablespoons refined avocado oil or macadamia nut oil
- Finely ground gray sea salt and ground black pepper
- 2 tablespoons chopped fresh parsley, for garnish

1. Prepare the cabbage: Place ¼ cup (60 ml) of avocado oil and the red onions in a large frying pan over medium heat. Sauté the onions for 5 minutes. Add the sliced cabbage and continue to cook for 5 minutes, or until lightly wilted. Add the wine, bone broth, vinegar, salt, and pepper. Cover, reduce the heat to medium-low, and cook for 25 minutes. During the last 5 minutes of cooking, remove the lid and continue to cook, uncovered, to allow some of the juices to evaporate.
2. Meanwhile, place an oven rack in the top position and set the broiler to low. (If your oven doesn't have a low broil setting, just "broil" is fine.)
3. Divide the cabbage among 4 plates, top each plate with a salmon steak, and serve garnished with parsley.

PER SERVING

Calories: 485 | Fat: 34.5g | Carbs: 8.3g | Dietary Fiber: 3.3g | Net Carbs: 5g | Sugars: 4.4g | Protein: 35.2g

Chapter 8

Vegan and Vegetarian

Herbed Pumpkin

Prep time: 15 minutes | Cook time: 7 to 8 Hours | Serves 6

- 3 tablespoons extra-virgin olive oil, divided
- 1 pound pumpkin, cut into 1-inch chunks
- ½ cup coconut milk
- 1 tablespoon apple cider vinegar
- ½ teaspoon chopped thyme
- 1 teaspoon chopped oregano
- ¼ teaspoon salt
- 1 cup greek yogurt

1. Lightly grease the insert of the slow cooker with 1 tablespoon of the olive oil.
2. Add the remaining 2 tablespoons of the olive oil with the pumpkin, coconut milk, apple cider vinegar, thyme, oregano, and salt to the insert.
3. Cover and cook on low for 7 to 8 hours.
4. Mash the pumpkin with the yogurt using a potato masher until smooth.
5. Serve warm.

PER SERVING

Calories: 158|Total Fat: 13g|Protein: 5g|Total Carbs: 8g|Fiber: 3g|Net Carbs: 5g|Cholesterol: 2mg

Tofu & Vegetable Stir-Fry

Prep time: 10 minutes| Cook time: 8 minutes | Serves 4

- 2 tbsp olive oil
- 1 ½ cups extra firm tofu, cubed
- 1 ½ tbsp flax seed meal
- Salt and black pepper, to taste
- 1 garlic clove, minced
- 1 cup mushrooms, sliced
- 1 tbsp sesame seeds

1. In a bowl, add onion powder, tofu, salt, soy sauce, black pepper, flaxseed, and garlic. Toss the mixture to coat and allow to marinate for 20-30 minutes.
2. In a pan, warm oil over medium heat, add in broccoli, mushrooms and tofu mixture and stir-fry for 6-8 minutes. Serve sprinkled with sesame seeds.

PER SERVING

Calories: 423 | Fat 31g | Net Carbs: 7.3g | Protein 25g

Simple Spaghetti Squash

Prep time: 15 minutes | Cook time: 6 hours | Serves 8

- 1 small spaghetti squash, washed
- ½ cup chicken stock
- ¼ cup butter
- salt, for seasoning
- freshly ground black pepper, for seasoning

1. Place the squash and chicken stock in the insert of the slow cooker. The squash should not touch the sides of the insert.
2. Cook on low for 6 hours.
3. Let the squash cool for 10 minutes and cut in half.
4. Season with salt and pepper and serve.

PER SERVING

Calories: 98|Total Fat: 7g|Protein: 1g|Total Carbs: 6g|Fiber: 3g|Net Carbs: 3g|Cholesterol: 15mg

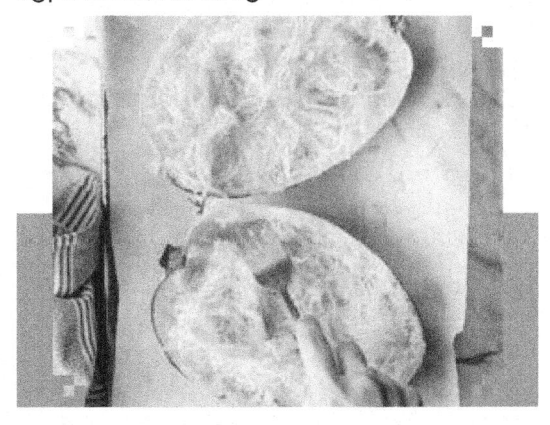

The XXL Keto Diet Cookbook

Kale with Bacon

Prep time: 15 minutes | Cook time: 6 Hours | Serves 8

- 2 tablespoons bacon fat
- 2 pounds kale, rinsed and chopped roughly
- 12 bacon slices, cooked and chopped
- 2 teaspoons minced garlic
- 2 cups vegetable broth
- salt, for seasoning
- freshly ground black pepper, for seasoning

1. Generously grease the insert of the slow cooker with the bacon fat.
2. Add the kale, bacon, garlic, and broth to the insert. Gently toss to mix.
3. Cover and cook on low for 6 hours.
4. Season with salt and pepper, and serve hot.

PER SERVING

Calories: 147|Total Fat: 10g|Protein: 7g|Total Carbs: 7g|Fiber: 3g|Net Carbs: 4g|Cholesterol: 17mg

Golden Mushrooms

Prep time: 10 minutes | Cook time: 6 Hours | Serves 8

- 3 tablespoons extra-virgin olive oil
- 1 pound button mushrooms, wiped clean and halved
- 2 teaspoons minced garlic
- ¼ teaspoon salt
- ⅛ teaspoon freshly ground black pepper
- 2 tablespoons chopped fresh parsley

1. Place The Olive Oil, Mushrooms, Garlic, Salt, and Pepper In The Insert Of The Slow Cooker and Toss To Coat.
2. Cover and Cook on Low For 6 Hours.
3. Serve Tossed with The Parsley.

PER SERVING

Calories: 58|Total Fat: 5g|Protein: 2g|Total Carbs: 2g|Fiber: 1g|Net Carbs: 1g|Cholesterol: 0mg

Marinated Portobello Mushrooms

Prep time: 5 minutes, plus 30 minutes to marinate | Cook time: 15 minutes | Serves 2

- 2 large portobello mushroom caps
- 3 tablespoons extra-virgin olive oil
- 1 tablespoon balsamic vinegar (no sugar added)
- 1 tablespoon minced fresh parsley
- ½ teaspoon granulated erythritol
- ½ teaspoon kosher salt
- ½ teaspoon minced garlic
- ⅛ teaspoon ground black pepper
- ⅛ teaspoon red pepper flakes

1. Remove the stems from the mushroom caps and scrape off the inside ribs with a spoon. Slice the mushrooms into ¼-inch strips.
2. Place the oil, vinegar, parsley, sweetener, salt, garlic, black pepper, and red pepper flakes in a medium-sized bowl and whisk until fully combined. Add the mushrooms to the marinade and gently fold with a rubber spatula to coat the strips completely, being careful not to break the mushrooms into small pieces.
3. Marinate at room temperature for at least 30 minutes or up to 2 hours. Store in an airtight container in the refrigerator for up to 3 days.

PER SERVING

Calories: 204 | Fat: 21g | Protein: 2g | Carbs: 3.5g | Fiber: 1g | Net Carbs: 2.5g

Cheesy Cauliflower Puree

Prep time: 5 minutes | Cook time: 14 minutes | Serves 4

- 5 cups raw cauliflower florets
- 2 tablespoons heavy whipping cream
- 1 tablespoon butter, plus more for serving if desired
- ½ teaspoon kosher salt
- ¼ teaspoon ground black pepper
- ⅛ teaspoon garlic powder
- ¼ cup shredded Dubliner or other sharp cheddar cheese

1. Place the cauliflower, cream, butter, salt, pepper, and garlic powder in a large microwave-safe bowl. Microwave, uncovered, on high for 6 minutes. Remove the bowl and stir well.
2. Return the bowl to the microwave and cook on high for another 8 minutes (again uncovered), or until the cauliflower is fork-tender. Remove the bowl from the microwave and transfer the cauliflower mixture to a blender or food processor.
3. Add the cheese and puree for 2 minutes, or until smooth, scraping the sides as necessary to puree all of the cauliflower. Taste and season with salt and pepper, if desired. Serve immediately, topped with more butter if you like.
4. Store in an airtight container in the refrigerator for up to 5 days. To reheat, microwave on high for 2 minutes per cup of puree. Stir and serve.

PER SERVING

Calories: 145 | Fat: 11g | Protein: 6g | Carbs: 8g | Fiber: 4g | Net Carbs: 4g

Hot Pizza with Tomatoes, Cheese & Olives

Prep time: 30 minutes | Cook time: 20 minutes |Serves 2

- 2 tbsp psyllium husk
- 1 cup cheddar cheese
- 2 tbsp cream cheese
- 2 tbsp Pecorino cheese
- 1 tsp oregano
- ½ cup almond flour
- Topping
- 1 tomato, sliced
- 4 oz cheddar cheese, sliced
- ¼ cup tomato sauce
- 1 jalapeño pepper, sliced
- ½ cup black olives
- 2 tbsp basil, chopped

1. Preheat the oven to 375 F.
2. Microwave the cheddar cheese in an oven-proof bowl. In a separate bowl, combine cream cheese, pecorino cheese, psyllium husk, almond flour, and oregano. Add in the melted cheddar cheese and mix with your hands to combine.
3. Divide the dough in two. Roll out the two crusts in circles and place on a lined baking sheet.
4. Bake for about 10 minutes.
5. Spread the tomato sauce over the crust and top with the cheddar cheese slices, jalapeño pepper, and tomato slices. Return to the oven and bake for another 10 minutes.
6. Garnish with black olives and basil.

PER SERVING

Calories: 576 | Fat: 42.3g | Net Carbs: 7.5g | Protein 32.4g

Secret Stuffed Peppers

Prep time: 10 minutes | **Cook time:** 45 minutes | Serves 1

- 4 ounces (115 g) chicken livers
- 1 tablespoon apple cider vinegar
- 1 pound (455 g) ground beef
- ¼ cup (60 ml) avocado oil, or ¼ cup (55 g) coconut oil or ghee
- 1 small red onion, diced
- 6 cloves garlic, minced
- 1½ teaspoons ground black pepper
- 1 teaspoon dried oregano leaves
- ½ teaspoon finely ground sea salt
- 4 medium bell peppers, any color
- 1 cup (125 g) riced cauliflower
- 1 cup (140 g) shredded cheddar cheese (dairy-free or regular), divided

1. Soak the livers: Place the livers in a medium-sized bowl and cover with water. Add the vinegar. Cover and place in the fridge to soak for 24 to 48 hours.
2. After at least 24 hours, rinse and drain the soaked livers, then chop them into very small pieces with either a knife or a sharp pair of scissors.
3. Place the livers in a large frying pan along with the ground beef, oil, onion, garlic, black pepper, oregano, and salt. Sauté over medium heat until no longer pink, about 15 minutes, stirring often to crumble the meat as it cooks.
4. Meanwhile, cut the tops off the bell peppers, then core them, being sure to remove all the seeds and white membranes.
5. Place the peppers right side up in an 8-inch (20-cm) square baking pan and preheat the oven to 350°F (177°C).
6. After the meat mixture has cooked for 15 minutes, toss in the riced cauliflower and ¾ cup (105 g) of the cheese and stir to combine. Spoon the mixture into the peppers, dividing it evenly. Then sprinkle the tops with the remaining cheese, 1 tablespoon per pepper.
7. Bake for 25 to 30 minutes, until the peppers have softened and the cheese has melted. Enjoy!

PER SERVING

Calories: 573 | Fat: 41 g | Carbs: 11.8 g | Dietary Fiber: 7.6 g | Net Carbs: 4.2 g | Sugars: 1.6 g | Protein: 39.4 g

Greek Salad with Poppy Seed Dressing

Prep time: 3 hours 15 minutes | **Cook time:** 5 minutes | Serves 4

- For The Dressing
- 1 cup poppy seeds
- 2 cups water
- 2 tbsp green onions, chopped
- 1 garlic clove, minced
- lime, freshly squeezed
- tbsp almond milk
- For The Salad
- 1 head lettuce, separated into leaves
- 3 tomatoes, diced
- 3 cucumbers, sliced
- 2 tbsp kalamata olives, pitted

1. Put all dressing ingredients, except for the poppy seeds, in a food processor and pulse until well incorporated. Add in poppy seeds and mix well with a fork. Mix and divide salad ingredients between 4 plates.
2. Add the dressing to each and shake to serve.

PER SERVING

Calories: 208 | Fat: 15.6g | Net Carbs: 6.7g | Protein: 7.6g

Sweet-Braised Red Cabbage

Prep time: 15 minutes | Cook time: 7 to 8 Hours | Serves 8

- 1 tablespoon extra-virgin olive oil
- 1 small red cabbage, coarsely shredded (about 6 cups)
- ½ sweet onion, thinly sliced
- ¼ cup apple cider vinegar
- 3 tablespoons granulated erythritol
- 2 teaspoons minced garlic
- ½ teaspoon ground nutmeg
- ⅛ teaspoon ground cloves
- 2 tablespoons butter
- salt, for seasoning
- freshly ground black pepper, for seasoning
- ½ cup chopped walnuts, for garnish
- ½ cup crumbled blue cheese, for garnish
- pink peppercorns, for garnish (optional)

1. Lightly Grease the Insert of The Slow Cooker with The Olive Oil.
2. Add The Cabbage, Onion, Apple Cider Vinegar, Erythritol, Garlic, Nutmeg, and Cloves to The Insert, Stirring to Mix Well.
3. Break Off Little Slices of Butter and Scatter Them on Top of The Cabbage Mixture.
4. Cover and Cook on Low For 7 To 8 Hours.
5. Season with Salt and Pepper.
6. Serve Topped with The Walnuts, Blue Cheese, and Peppercorns (If Desired).

PER SERVING:

Calories: 152|Total Fat: 12g|Protein: 7g|Total Carbs: 4g|Fiber: 1g|Net Carbs: 3g|Cholesterol: 13mg

Mozzarella & Bell Pepper Avocado Cups

Prep time: 10 minutes | Cook time: 5 minutes |Serves 4

- 2 avocados
- ½ cup fresh mozzarella, chopped
- 2 tbsp olive oil
- 2 cups green bell peppers, chopped
- 1 onion, chopped
- ½ tsp garlic puree
- Salt and black pepper, to taste
- ½ tomato, chopped
- 2 tbsp basil, chopped

1. Halve the avocados and scoop out 2 teaspoons of flesh; set aside.
2. Sauté olive oil, garlic, onion, and bell peppers in a skillet over medium heat for 5 minutes until tender.
3. Remove to a bowl and leave to cool. Mix in the reserved avocado, tomato, salt, mozzarella, and black pepper. Fill the avocado halves with the mixture and serve sprinkled with basil.

PER SERVING

Calories: 273 | Fat 22.5g | Net Carbs: 6.9g | Protein 8.3g

Smoked Vegetable Bake with Parmesan

Prep time: 35 minutes | Cook time: 30 minutes | Serves 4

- 2 tbsp olive oil
- 1 onion, chopped
- 1 celery, chopped
- 2 carrots, sliced
- ½ pound artichokes, halved
- 1 cup vegetable broth
- 1 tsp turmeric
- Salt and black pepper, to taste
- ½ tsp liquid smoke
- 1 cup Parmesan cheese, shredded
- 2 tbsp chives, chopped

1. Preheat oven to 360 F and grease a baking dish with olive oil. Place in the artichokes, onion, and celery. Combine vegetable broth with turmeric, black pepper, liquid smoke, and salt.
2. Spread this mixture over the vegetables and bake for 25 minutes. Sprinkle with Parmesan cheese and return in the oven to bake for 5 minutes. Decorate with fresh chives and serve.

PER SERVING

Calories: 231 | Fat 15.5g | Net Carbs: 9.3g | Protein 11g

Sweet Sesame Glazed Bok Choy

Prep time: 5 minutes | Cook time: 17 minutes | Serves 4

- 1 pound baby bok choy (see note)
- ¼ cup filtered water
- 3 tablespoons granulated erythritol
- 3 tablespoons unseasoned rice wine vinegar
- 3 tablespoons wheat-free soy sauce
- ½ teaspoon toasted sesame oil
- 1 tablespoon red pepper flakes
- ½ teaspoon xanthan gum
- 1 tablespoon sesame seeds, for garnish

1. Place the bok choy in a large microwave-safe bowl and add about ½ cup of water. Cover with plastic wrap and microwave on high for 5 minutes.
2. Remove the bowl from the microwave and uncover. Rinse the bok choy in cold water to stop the cooking process, then drain and set aside.
3. Place the water, sweetener, vinegar, soy sauce, and sesame oil in a large sauté pan and whisk until well blended. Cook over medium heat for 5 minutes, or until reduced by half.
4. Add the red pepper flakes and xanthan gum to the sauce and continue cooking, stirring occasionally, until the sauce has thickened enough to coat the back of a spoon, about 5 more minutes.
5. Add the bok choy to the sauce and stir gently to coat. Cook for 2 minutes, or until the bok choy is heated through. Garnish with sesame seeds and serve.

PER SERVING

Calories: 45 | Fat: 2g | Protein: 4g | Carbs: 4.5g | Fiber: 2.5g | Net Carbs: 2g

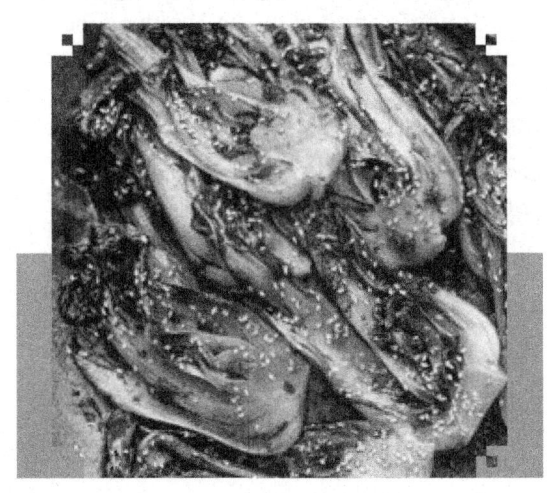

Chapter 9

Soups, Stew and Salads

Chinese Tofu Soup

Prep time: 15 minutes | Cook time: 7 minutes | Serves 4

- 4 cups chicken stock
- 1 tbsp soy sauce, sugar-free
- 2 spring onions, sliced
- 1 tsp sesame oil, softened
- 2 eggs, beaten
- 1-inch piece ginger, grated
- Salt and black ground, to taste
- ½ pound extra-firm tofu, cubed
- A handful of fresh cilantro, chopped

1. Boil in a pan over medium heat, soy sauce, chicken stock and sesame oil. Place in eggs as you whisk to incorporate completely.
2. Change heat to low and add salt, spring onions, black pepper and ginger; cook for 5
3. minutes. Place in tofu and simmer for 1 to 2 minutes.
4. Divide into soup bowls and serve sprinkled with fresh cilantro.

PER SERVING

Calories: 163 | Fat 10g | Net Carbs: 2.4g | Protein 14.5g

Spanish-Style Tomato Soup

Prep time: 15 minutes | Cook time: 5 minutes | Serves 6

- 2 small green peppers, roasted
- 2 large red peppers, roasted
- 2 avocados, flesh scoped out
- 2 garlic cloves
- 2 spring onions, chopped
- 1 cucumber, chopped
- 1 cup olive oil
- 2 tbsp lemon juice
- 4 tomatoes, chopped
- 7 ounces goat cheese
- 1 small red onion, chopped
- 2 tbsp apple cider vinegar
- Salt to taste

1. Place the peppers, tomatoes, avocado, spring onions, garlic, lemon juice, olive oil, vinegar, and salt in a food processor or a blender. Pulse until your desired consistency is reached.
2. Taste, and adjust the seasoning. Transfer the mixture to a pot. Stir in cucumbers and red onion.
3. Cover and chill in the fridge at least 2 hours. Divide the soup between 6 bowls. Serve very cold, generously topped with goat cheese and an extra drizzle of olive oil.

PER SERVING

Calories: 528 | Net Carbs: 8.5g | Fat: 45.8g | Protein 7.5g

Creamy Coconut Soup with Chicken & Celery

Prep time: 25 minutes | Cook time: 18 minutes | Serves 4

- 3 tbsp butter
- 1 onion, chopped
- 2 chicken breasts, chopped
- Salt and black pepper, to taste
- ½ cup coconut cream
- ¼ cup celery, chopped

1. Warm butter in a pot over medium heat. Sauté the onion and celery for 3 minutes. Stir in chicken, 4 cups of water, salt and pepper, and simmer for 15 minutes.
2. Pour in the coconut cream and stir.

PER SERVING

Calories: 394 | Fat: 24.2g | Net Carbs: 6.1g | Protein 29.5g

Cowboy Stew of Bacon, Cheese & Cauliflower

Prep time: 40 minutes | Cook time: 23 minutes | Serves 4

- 2 tbsp olive oil
- ½ cup mozzarella cheese, grated
- 1 cup chicken broth
- 1 garlic clove, minced
- 1 shallot, chopped
- Salt and black pepper, to taste
- ¼ cup heavy cream
- 1 pound bacon, chopped
- 1 head cauliflower, cut into florets
- 1 small carrot, chopped
- 1 tsp dried thyme
- 1 tbsp parsley, chopped

1. In a pot, heat the olive oil and sauté garlic and shallot for 3 minutes until soft. Add in the bacon and fry for 5 minutes. Then, pour in broth, carrot, and cauliflower and simmer for 10 minutes.
2. Stir in heavy cream and cheese and cook for 5 minutes. Season with thyme, salt, pepper, and parsley to serve.

PER SERVING

Calories: 713 | Fat: 61.2g | Net Carbs: 4.4g | Protein 32.4g

Baked Winter Pork Stew

Prep time: 40 minutes | Cook time: 40 minutes | Serves 4

- 3 tsp olive oil
- 1 pound ground pork
- 1 cup vegetable stock
- 14 oz canned tomatoes with juice
- 1 carrot, chopped
- 1 celery stick, chopped
- 1 lb butternut squash, chopped
- 1 tbsp Worcestershire sauce
- 2 bay leaves
- Salt and black pepper to taste
- 3 tbsp fresh parsley, chopped
- 1 onion, chopped
- 1 tsp dried sage
- 1 garlic clove, minced

1. Preheat oven to 360 F.
2. Warm olive oil over medium heat and add the onion, garlic, celery, carrot, and ground pork.
3. Cook for 10 minutes, stirring often until no longer pink.
4. Add in butternut squash, Worcestershire sauce, bay leaves, vegetable stock, canned tomatoes, and sage, and bring to a boil. Reduce heat, cover, and simmer for 20 minutes.
5. Adjust the seasonings.
6. Remove and discard the bay leaves and transfer to a baling casserole. Bake in the oven for 10 minutes until the top is golden brown. Serve sprinkled with parsley.

PER SERVING

Calories: 353 | Fat: 16.5g | Net Carbs: 6.6g | Protein 26.1g

Awesome Chicken Enchilada Soup

Prep time: 30 minutes | Cook time: 20 minutes |Serves 4

- 2 tbsp coconut oil
- 1 lb chicken thighs
- ¾ cup red enchilada sauce
- ¼ cup water
- ¼ cup onion, chopped
- 3 oz canned diced green chilis
- 1 avocado, sliced
- 1 cup cheddar cheese, shredded
- ¼ cup pickled jalapeños, chopped
- ½ cup sour cream
- 1 tomato, diced

1. Put a large pan over medium heat. Add coconut oil and warm. Place in the chicken and cook until browned on the outside. Stir in onion, chilies, water, and enchilada sauce, then close with a lid.
2. Allow simmering for 20 minutes until the chicken is cooked through. Spoon the soup on a serving bowl and top with the sauce, cheese, sour cream, tomato, and avocado.

PER SERVING

Calories: 643 | Fat: 44.2g | Net Carbs: 9.7g | Protein 45.8g

Creamy Broccoli and Bacon Soup

Prep time: 5 minutes | Cook time: 20 minutes |Serves 4

- 2 slices bacon, chopped
- 2 tablespoons scallions, chopped
- 1 carrot, chopped
- 1 celery, chopped
- Salt and ground black pepper, to taste
- 1 teaspoon garlic, finely chopped
- 1/2 teaspoon dried rosemary
- 1 sprig thyme, stripped and chopped
- 1/2 head green cabbage, shredded
- 1/2 head broccoli, broken into small florets
- 3 cups water
- 1 cup chicken stock
- 1/2 cup full-fat yogurt

1. Heat a stockpot over medium heat; now, sear the bacon until crisp. Reserve the bacon and 1 tablespoon of fat.
2. Then, cook scallions, carrots, and celery in 1 tablespoon of reserved fat. Add salt, pepper, and garlic; cook an additional 1 minute or until fragrant.
3. Now, stir in rosemary, thyme, cabbage, and broccoli. Pour in water and stock, bringing to a rapid boil; reduce heat and let it simmer for 10 minutes more.
4. Add yogurt and cook an additional 5 minutes, stirring occasionally. Use an immersion blender, to puree your soup until smooth.
5. Taste and adjust the seasonings. Garnish with the cooked bacon just before serving.

PER SERVING

Calories: 95 | Fat: 7.6g | Carbs: 4.1g | Fiber: 1g | Protein: 3g

Zucchini and Shallot Soup

Prep time: 5 minutes | Cook time: 20 minutes |Serves 3

- 2 teaspoons extra-virgin olive oil
- 1/2 pound zucchini, peeled and diced
- 1/2 shallot, chopped
- 1/2 cup celery, chopped
- 1/2 teaspoon garlic powder
- 1/4 teaspoon red pepper flakes
- 2 cups vegetable broth

1. Heat 1 teaspoon of the olive oil in a soup pot over medium-high heat; cook your zucchini for 1 to 2 minutes or until just tender; reserve.
2. In the same pot, heat the remaining teaspoon of olive oil; sauté the shallot until tender and translucent.
3. Add the remaining ingredients to the sautéed vegetables in the soup pot. Reduce the heat to medium-low, cover and let it cook for 15 minutes or until thoroughly heated.
4. Ladle into serving bowls and serve warm. Bon appétit!

PER SERVING

Calories: 58 | Fat: 3.3g | Carbs: 3.5g | Protein: 2.3g | Fiber: 1.2g

Grilled Tofu Kabobs with Arugula Salad

Prep time: 40 minutes | Cook time: 12 minutes | Serves 4

- 14 oz firm tofu, cut into strips
- 4 tsp sesame oil
- 1 lemon, juiced
- 5 tbsp soy sauce, sugar-free
- 3 tsp garlic powder
- 4 tbsp coconut flour
- ½ cup sesame seeds
- Arugula salad:
- 4 cups arugula, chopped
- 2 tsp extra virgin olive oil
- 2 tbsp pine nuts
- Salt and black pepper to season
- 1 tbsp balsamic vinegar

1. Stick the tofu strips on the skewers, height-wise and place onto a plate.
2. In a bowl, mix sesame oil, lemon juice, soy sauce, garlic powder, and coconut flour. Pour the soy sauce mixture over the tofu, and turn in the sauce to be adequately coated. Cover the dish with cling film and marinate in the fridge for 2 hours.
3. Heat the griddle pan over high heat. Coat the tofu in the sesame seeds and grill in the griddle pan to be golden brown on both sides, about 12 minutes in total.
4. Arrange the arugula on a serving plate. Drizzle over olive oil and balsamic vinegar, and season with salt and black pepper. Sprinkle with pine nuts and place the tofu kabobs on top to serve.

PER SERVING

Calories: 411 | Fat: 33g | Net Carbs: 7.1g | Protein 22g

Caprese Asparagus Salad

Prep time: 5 minutes | Cook time: 20 minutes | Serves 4

- 1 teaspoon fresh lime juice
- 1 tablespoon hot Hungarian paprika infused oil
- 1/2 teaspoon kosher salt
- 1/4 teaspoon red pepper flakes
- 1/2 pound asparagus spears, trimmed
- 1 cup grape tomatoes, halved
- 2 tablespoon red wine vinegar
- 1 garlic clove, pressed 1-2 drops liquid stevia
- 1 tablespoon fresh basil
- 1 tablespoon fresh chives
- 1/2 cup mozzarella, grated

1. Heat your grill to the hottest setting. Toss your asparagus with the lime juice, hot Hungarian paprika infused oil, salt, and red pepper flakes.
2. Place the asparagus spears on the hot grill. Grill until one side chars; then, grill your asparagus on the other side.
3. Top with freshly grated mozzarella cheese and serve immediately.

PER SERVING

Calories: 187 | Fat: 13.3g | Carbs: 7.4g | Protein: 9.5g | Fiber: 3.4g

Cilantro Shrimp Stew with Sriracha Sauce

Prep time: 25 minutes | Cook time: 10 minutes | Serves 6

- 1 cup coconut milk
- 2 tbsp lime juice
- ¼ cup diced roasted peppers
- 1 ½ pounds shrimp, peeled and deveined
- ¼ cup olive oil
- 1 garlic clove, minced
- 14 ounces diced tomatoes
- 2 tbsp sriracha sauce
- ¼ cup onions, chopped
- Salt and black pepper to taste

1. Heat the olive oil in a pot over medium heat. Add onions and, cook for 3 minutes, or until translucent. Add the garlic and cook, for another minute, until soft. Add tomatoes, shrimp, and cilantro.
2. Do NOT bring to a boil. Stir in the lime juice, and season with salt and pepper to taste. Spoon the stew in bowls, garnish with fresh dill, and serve warm.

PER SERVING

Calories: 324 | Net Carbs: 5g | Fat: 21g | Protein 23g

Stewed Turkey with Greens

Prep time: 30 minutes | Cook time: 23 minutes | Serves 4

- 1 onion, chopped
- 2 tbsp olive oil
- 4 cups leftover turkey meat, chopped
- 1 cup snow peas
- ½ tsp ground coriander
- 1 tsp cumin
- ¼ cup sour cream
- 1 tbsp cilantro, chopped

1. Heat olive oil in a pan over medium heat. Cook the onion and garlic for 3 minutes until soft.
2. Stir in the snow peas and chicken stock, and cook for 10 minutes.
3. Place in the turkey, ground coriander, salt, broccoli rabe, Jalapeño pepper, cumin, and black pepper, and cook for 10 minutes. Stir in the sour cream, top with chopped cilantro and serve.

PER SERVING

Calories: 443 | Fat: 28g | Net Carbs: 8.2g | Protein 36.4g

Almond Parsnip Soup with Sour Cream

Prep time: 25 minutes | Cook time: 21 minutes |Serves 4

- 1 tbsp olive oil
- 1 cup onion, chopped
- 1 celery, chopped
- 2 cloves garlic, minced
- 2 turnips, peeled and chopped
- 4 cups vegetable broth
- Salt and white pepper, to taste
- ¼ cup ground almonds
- 1 cup almond milk
- 1 tbsp fresh cilantro, chopped
- 4 tsp sour cream

1. Warm oil in a pot over medium heat and sauté celery, garlic, and onion for 6 minutes. Stir in white pepper, broth, salt, and ground almonds. Bring to the boil and simmer for 15 minutes.
2. Transfer soup to an immersion blender and puree. Serve garnished with sour cream and cilantro.

PER SERVING

Calories: 125 | Fat 7.1g | Net Carbs: 7.7g | Protein 4g

Cream of Cauliflower & Leek Soup

Prep time: 20 minutes | Cook time: 35 minutes |Serves 4

- 4 cups vegetable broth
- 2 heads cauliflower, cut into florets
- 1 celery stalk, chopped
- 1 onion, chopped
- 1 cup leeks, chopped
- 2 tbsp butter
- 1 tbsp olive oil
- 1 cup heavy cream
- ½ tsp red pepper flakes

1. Warm butter and olive oil in a pot set over medium heat and sauté onion, leeks, and celery for 5 minutes. Stir in vegetable broth and cauliflower and bring to a boil; simmer for 30 minutes.
2. Transfer the mixture to an immersion blender and puree; add in the heavy cream and stir. Decorate with red pepper flakes to serve.

PER SERVING

Calories: 255 | Fat 21g | Net Carbs: 5.3g | Protein 4.4g

Creamy Roasted Asparagus Salad

Prep time: 5 minutes | Cook time: 20 minutes |Serves 5

- 14 ounces asparagus spears, trimmed
- 2 tablespoons olive oil
- 1/2 teaspoon oregano
- 1/2 teaspoon rosemary
- Sea salt and freshly ground black pepper, to taste
- 5 tablespoons mayonnaise
- 3 tablespoons sour cream
- 1 tablespoon wine vinegar
- 1 teaspoon fresh garlic, minced
- 1 cup cherry tomatoes, halved

1. In a lightly greased roasting pan, toss the asparagus with the olive oil, oregano, rosemary, salt, and black pepper.
2. Roast in the preheated oven at 425 degrees F for 13 to 15 minutes until just tender.
3. Serve at room temperature. Bon appétit!

PER SERVING

Calories: 179 | Fat: 17.5g | Carbs: 4.7g | Protein: 2.5g | Fiber: 2g

The XXL Keto Diet Cookbook | 85

Three-Color Salad with Pesto Sauce

Prep time: 10 minutes | Cook time: 5 minutes | Serves 4

- 3 tomatoes, sliced
- 1 large avocado, sliced
- 8 kalamata olives
- ¼ pound buffalo mozzarella, sliced
- 2 tbsp pesto sauce
- 2 tbsp olive oil

1. Arrange the tomato slices on a serving platter. Place the avocado slices in the middle.
2. Arrange the olives around the avocado slices. Drop pieces of mozzarella on the platter.
3. Drizzle the pesto sauce all over, and drizzle olive oil as well.

PER SERVING

Calories: 290 | Net Carbs: 4.3g | Fat: 25g | Protein 9g

Grandma's Chicken Soup

Prep time: 5 minutes | Cook time: 30 minutes | Serves 2

- 2 chicken drumsticks, skinless and boneless
- 1/2 white onion, chopped
- 1 stalk celery, chopped
- 1 teaspoon poultry seasoning mix
- 1 tablespoon fresh cilantro, chopped

1. Place the chicken in a stockpot. Add enough water to cover by about an inch.
2. Now, add in the chopped onion, celery and poultry seasoning mix. Bring to a boil over medium-high heat. Turn the temperature to medium-low and cook for 35 to 40 minutes.
3. As for the chicken, the meat thermometer should register 165 degrees F. Make sure to add extra water during the cooking as needed to keep the ingredients covered.
4. Season to taste and serve with fresh cilantro. Bon appétit!

PER SERVING

Calories: 166 | Fat: 4.9g | Carbs: 3.3g | Protein: 25.6g | Fiber: 0.7g

Asian-Style Turkey Soup

Prep time: 5 minutes | Cook time: 20 minutes | Serves 5

- 2 tablespoons canola oil
- 2 Oriental sweets peppers, deseeded and chopped
- 1 Bird's eye chili, deseeded and chopped
- 2 green onions, chopped
- 5 cups vegetable broth
- 1 pound turkey thighs, deboned and cut into halves
- 1/2 teaspoon five-spice powder
- 1 teaspoon oyster sauce
- Kosher salt, to taste

1. Heat the olive oil in a stockpot over a moderate flame. Then, sauté the peppers and onions until they have softened or about 4 minutes
2. Add in the other ingredients and bring to a boil. Turn the heat to simmer, cover, and continue to cook an additional 12 minutes.
3. Ladle into individual bowls and serve warm. Enjoy!

PER SERVING

Calories: 180 | Fat: 7.5g | Carbs: 6.7g | Protein: 21.4g | Fiber: 1.2g

Red Wine & Pork Stew

Prep time: 1 hour 25 minutes | Cook time: 65 minutes |Serves 4

- 2 tbsp olive oil
- 1 pound pork stew meat, cubed
- Salt and black pepper, to taste
- 1 red pepper, minced
- 1 garlic clove, minced
- 1 onion, chopped
- ½ cup beef stock
- ¼ cup red wine
- 1 carrot, chopped
- 1 small cabbage head, shredded
- 2 tbsp chives, chopped
- ½ cup sour cream
- 1 tbsp oregano, chopped

1. Sear the pork in warm olive oil over medium heat until brown. Add garlic, onion, red pepper, chives and carrot; sauté for 5 minutes. Pour in the cabbage, beef stock and red wine, and bring to a boil.
2. Reduce the heat and cook for 1 hour while covered. Add in the sour cream as you stir for 1 minute, adjust the seasonings and serve sprinkled with oregano.

PER SERVING

Calories: 367 | Fat: 15g | Net Carbs: 7.6g | Protein 38g

Mushroom Cream Soup with Herbs

Prep time: 25 minutes | Cook time: 23 minutes |Serves 4

- 1 onion, chopped
- ½ cup crème fraiche
- ¼ cup butter
- 12 oz white mushrooms, chopped
- 1 tsp thyme leaves, chopped
- 1 tsp parsley leaves, chopped
- 2 garlic cloves, minced
- 4 cups vegetable broth
- Salt and black pepper, to taste

1. Add butter, onion and garlic to a pot over high heat and cook for 3 minutes. Add in mushrooms, salt and pepper, and cook for 10 minutes. Pour in broth and bring to a boil.
2. Reduce heat and simmer for 10 minutes. Puree soup with a hand blender. Stir in crème fraiche. Garnish with herbs before serving.

PER SERVING

Calories: 213 | Fat: 18g | Net Carbs: 4.1g | Protein 3.1g

Old-Fashioned Chicken Salad

Prep time: 5 minutes | Cook time: 20 minutes |Serves 4

- Poached Chicken
- 2 chicken breasts, skinless and boneless
- 1/2 teaspoon salt
- 2 bay laurels
- 1 teaspoon Dijon mustard
- 2 teaspoons freshly squeezed lemon juice
- 1 cup mayonnaise, preferably homemade

1. Place all ingredients for the poached chicken in a stockpot; cover with water and bring to a rolling boil.
2. Turn the heat to medium-low and let it simmer for about 15 minutes or until a meat thermometer reads 165 degrees F. Let the poached chicken cool to room temperature.
3. Cut into strips and transfer to a nice salad bowl.

PER SERVING

Calories: 536 | Fat: 49g | Carbs: 3.1g | Protein: 19g | Fiber: 0.5g

Appendix 1 Measurement Conversion Chart

Volume Equivalents (Dry)	
US STANDARD	METRIC (APPROXIMATE)
1/8 teaspoon	0.5 mL
1/4 teaspoon	1 mL
1/2 teaspoon	2 mL
3/4 teaspoon	4 mL
1 teaspoon	5 mL
1 tablespoon	15 mL
1/4 cup	59 mL
1/2 cup	118 mL
3/4 cup	177 mL
1 cup	235 mL
2 cups	475 mL
3 cups	700 mL
4 cups	1 L

Volume Equivalents (Liquid)		
US STANDARD	US STANDARD (OUNCES)	METRIC (APPROXIMATE)
2 tablespoons	1 fl.oz.	30 mL
1/4 cup	2 fl.oz.	60 mL
1/2 cup	4 fl.oz.	120 mL
1 cup	8 fl.oz.	240 mL
1 1/2 cup	12 fl.oz.	355 mL
2 cups or 1 pint	16 fl.oz.	475 mL
4 cups or 1 quart	32 fl.oz.	1 L
1 gallon	128 fl.oz.	4 L

Temperatures Equivalents	
FAHRENHEIT(F)	CELSIUS(C) APPROXIMATE
225 °F	107 °C
250 °F	120 ° °C
275 °F	135 °C
300 °F	150 °C
325 °F	160 °C
350 °F	180 °C
375 °F	190 °C
400 °F	205 °C
425 °F	220 °C
450 °F	235 °C
475 °F	245 °C
500 °F	260 °C

Weight Equivalents	
US STANDARD	METRIC (APPROXIMATE)
1 ounce	28 g
2 ounces	57 g
5 ounces	142 g
10 ounces	284 g
15 ounces	425 g
16 ounces (1 pound)	455 g
1.5 pounds	680 g
2 pounds	907 g

Appendix 2 The Dirty Dozen and Clean Fifteen

The Environmental Working Group (EWG) is a nonprofit, nonpartisan organization dedicated to protecting human health and the environment Its mission is to empower people to live healthier lives in a healthier environment. This organization publishes an annual list of the twelve kinds of produce, in sequence, that have the highest amount of pesticide residue-the Dirty Dozen-as well as a list of the fifteen kinds of produce that have the least amount of pesticide residue-the Clean Fifteen.

THE DIRTY DOZEN

The 2016 Dirty Dozen includes the following produce. These are considered among the year's most important produce to buy organic:

Strawberries	Spinach
Apples	Tomatoes
Nectarines	Bell peppers
Peaches	Cherry tomatoes
Celery	Cucumbers
Grapes	Kale/collard greens
Cherries	Hot peppers

The Dirty Dozen list contains two additional items kale/collard greens and hot peppers-because they tend to contain trace levels of highly hazardous pesticides.

THE CLEAN FIFTEEN

The least critical to buy organically are the Clean Fifteen list. The following are on the 2016 list:

Avocados	Papayas
Corn	Kiw
Pineapples	Eggplant
Cabbage	Honeydew
Sweet peas	Grapefruit
Onions	Cantaloupe
Asparagus	Cauliflower
Mangos	

Some of the sweet corn sold in the United States are made from genetically engineered (GE) seedstock. Buy organic varieties of these crops to avoid GE produce.

Appendix 3 Index

A

almond 14, 15, 17, 18, 19, 23, 24, 26
apple 16, 20, 25, 31, 50, 54, 63, 65, 73, 76, 77, 80
apple cider vinegar 16, 20, 25, 31, 50, 54
asparagus 66, 84, 85
avocado 14, 16, 17, 21, 22, 23, 26, 27, 36

B

bacon 15, 17, 22, 24, 25, 29, 36, 46, 51, 55, 59
balsamic vinegar 55, 71, 74, 83
basil 44, 48, 60, 63, 75, 77, 84
bell pepper 15, 27, 42, 44, 47, 70
broccoli 36, 51, 52, 73, 82, 84
buns 26, 58
butter 14, 18, 19, 25, 27, 29, 30, 32

C

canola oil 86
carrot 16, 81, 82, 87
cauliflower 20, 36, 49, 57, 65, 67, 75, 76, 81, 85
cayenne 17, 29, 37, 50, 66
cayenne pepper 17, 29, 37, 50, 66
Cheddar cheese 51
cheese 16, 17, 18, 19, 23, 27, 29, 30, 31, 32
chives 16, 24, 36, 78, 84, 87

cinnamon 15, 18, 19, 23, 26, 37, 55, 59
coconut 14, 15, 16, 18, 20, 21, 23
coriander 43, 84
cumin 43, 55, 56, 63, 84

D

Dijon mustard 57, 67, 69, 71, 87

E

egg 16, 17, 19, 21, 22, 24, 25, 26, 29, 31

F

fish 66, 67, 68, 69, 71
flour 15, 17, 18, 24, 26, 27, 29, 31, 32
fresh chives 24, 78, 84
fresh cilantro 21, 33, 43, 51, 63, 70, 80, 85, 86
fresh parsley 20, 22, 25, 27, 35, 59

G

garlic 16, 21, 22, 26, 27, 29, 34, 35, 41, 42
garlic powder 22, 26, 27, 29, 34, 51, 52, 61
Greek yogurt 36

J

juice 27, 36, 38, 43, 45, 48, 56, 57, 59, 63, 65, 68, 69, 71, 80

K

kale 74
ketchup 19, 58
kosher salt 26, 33, 35, 67, 74, 75, 84

L

lemon 27, 32, 36, 38, 43, 44, 48, 55
lemon juice 27, 36, 38, 43, 48, 56, 63, 65
lime 45, 50, 70, 71, 76, 84
lime juice 45, 71, 84
lime zest 50

M

milk 14, 15, 17, 18, 19, 20, 23, 24, 31
Mozzarella 77
mushroom 74
mustard 49, 57, 58, 67, 69, 71, 87

N

nutmeg 70, 72
Nuts 79

O

olive oil 17, 21, 23, 24, 26, 29
onion 14, 17, 20, 22, 24, 25, 26, 31, 33
onion powder 25, 31, 38, 41, 48, 52, 53, 60, 82
oregano 31, 32, 36, 38, 41, 44, 47, 48, 51, 68

P

paprika 14, 31, 37, 41, 44, 48, 49
Parmesan cheese 14, 49, 57, 72, 79, 87
parsley 14, 17, 24, 25, 30, 39, 48
pasta 38, 70
pizza 73
potato 16, 69, 72

R

red pepper flakes 25, 30, 31, 35
rice 22, 34, 52
rosemary 21, 24, 33, 34, 35, 38, 42, 44, 68

S

salt 14, 15, 33, 35, 39, 66,
Sauce 33, 55, 61
soy sauce 25, 31, 33, 35, 39, 66, 68, 71, 85
sugar 16, 17, 18, 26, 33

T

tomato 26, 33, 37, 39, 45, 73
tortillas 27, 42, 58, 60

V

vinegar 16, 20, 25, 31, 38

W

white wine 48, 52, 56

Y

yogurt 30, 31, 33, 36, 73, 82

Z

zucchini 30, 42, 66, 83

Debra P. Johnson